KF 380. S63

D1131508

SOCIAL SCIENCE APPROACHES TO THE JUDICIAL PROCESS

A Symposium

SYMPOSIA ON LAW AND SOCIETY

GENERAL EDITOR: LEONARD W. LEVY

Claremont Graduate School

SOCIAL SCIENCE APPROACHES TO THE JUDICIAL PROCESS

A Symposium

JOEL B. GROSSMAN

WALTER F. MURPHY

SAMUEL KRISLOV

JOSEPH TANENHAUS

FRED KORT

LON L. FULLER

VON CANON LIBRARY
SOUTHERN SEMINARY
BUENA VISTA, VIRGINIA 24416

25138

DA CAPO PRESS • NEW YORK • 1971

The papers contained in this volume appeared originally in the *Harvard Law Review,* Volume 79, Number 8 (June 1966). They are reprinted by permission of the Editors of the *Harvard Law Review* and by arrangement with the contributors.

Library of Congress Catalog Card Number 74-153371

SBN 306-70135-9

Copyright © 1966 by The Harvard Law Review Association, Cambridge, Massachusetts

Published by Da Capo Press, Inc.

A Subsidiary of Plenum Publishing Corporation

227 West 17th Street, New York, N.Y. 10011

All Rights Reserved

Manufactured in the United States of America

CONTENTS

SOCIAL SCIENCE APPROACHES TO THE JUDICIAL PROCESS

A Symposium

Political scientists have recently begun to investigate new dimensions of the judicial process. While not unconcerned with the logical and normative aspects of judicial doctrine — the analysis of which has provided the main content of constitutional law inquiry in both law school and liberal arts curricula — their studies have focused particularly on the social and personal dimensions of judicial action. Developing in the spirit and with the methods and goals of the "social" sciences, these studies have been concerned more with the informal workings of groups and the behavior of political actors than with the formal structures of institutions. Their concepts and methods have stressed the need for reliability and precision in the gathering and processing of data, at a cost of ignoring some types of intuitive and perhaps more colorful explanations of random events. Various types of models or conceptual schemes have been devised purporting to depict the key relationships comprising the judicial process, and a heavy reliance has been placed on quantitative methods of analysis ("jurimetrics").

The articles that follow survey and review the work that has been done in several of these new spheres of inquiry. The authors were asked to describe representative research in a particular field and examine critically the basic assumptions, results, and potential of such research.

SOCIAL BACKGROUNDS AND JUDICIAL DECISION–MAKING

Joel B. Grossman *

I

LEGAL scholars and social scientists, having long since disabused themselves of the aesthetically pleasing but inaccurate view of the appellate judge's task as primarily mechanical and syllogistic,[1] are still seeking answers to the elusive question: to what extent is a judge a creature or a captive of personal values

---

* Assistant Professor of Political Science, University of Wisconsin. Fellow in Law and Political Science, Harvard Law School, 1965–1966. A.B., Queens College, 1957; M.A., University of Iowa, 1960, Ph.D., 1963.

[1] See, *e.g.*, CARDOZO, THE NATURE OF THE JUDICIAL PROCESS (1921); FRANK, LAW AND THE MODERN MIND (1930); Holmes, *The Path of the Law*, 10 HARV. L. REV. 457 (1897).

and attitudes developed during his prejudicial experiences? If it can be assumed that the task of judging — particularly on the Supreme Court of the United States — involves some very practical choices between policy alternatives, and if it can be further assumed that no judge derives all his premises from the courtroom, the sources of these "other" premises and the manner in which they affect the mix of personal and institutional factors which constitute the judicial function must yet be ascertained.

Assessing the role of personal values and experiences in judicial decisions is particularly difficult because of norms which prevent judges from openly casting their decisions in such terms.[2] Yet the inescapable conclusion that judicial decisions — and particularly constitutional law decisions — are at least partially attributable to the personal values and experiences of the judges impels a search beyond mere surface observations.[3]

Efforts to understand and explain judicial behavior in the light of the social backgrounds and experiences of the judges have been a staple of traditional descriptive and biographical studies, but it is only in the past decade that more systematic and theoretically oriented explorations have taken place. While sharing with traditional studies the judicial realists' assumptions about the dynamics of the judicial function, these explorations differ substantially in other respects. They are more concerned with general behavior patterns than with discrete actions or events and therefore tend to focus on properties of behavior which are amenable to generalization — for example, on judges' votes rather than on their opinions. They rely on methods of inquiry which assume that a useful way to examine judicial behavior is to consider the judge not as sui generis, but rather as a variety of *homo politicus*. Such a perspective is not to be confused with the exaggerated notion that judges are *no* different from other political actors.[4] It has the advantage, however, of permitting observations about judicial behavior to be integrated into broader-based studies of human behavior and legal-political institutions.

---

[2] One famous exception is Justice Frankfurter's denial that his Jewish immigrant background should result in a contrary vote. West Virginia State Bd. of Educ. v. Barnette, 319 U.S. 624, 646–47 (1943) (dissenting opinion).

[3] *Cf.* Haines, *General Observations on the Effects of Personal, Political, and Economic Influences in the Decisions of Judges*, 17 ILL. L. REV. 96 (1922).

[4] *Cf.* FRANK, COURTS ON TRIAL 254 (1949); Frankfurter, *The Judicial Process and the Supreme Court*, 98 PROCEEDINGS OF THE AMERICAN PHILOSOPHICAL SOCIETY 233 (1954).

All research must be understood and interpreted in the light of the organizing principles to which it subscribes. The ultimate goals of social science involve the construction of sophisticated theories of human behavior, in which judicial processes occupy a small but important part. Such theories emphasize systematic formulations of empirical data and place a high premium on generalization and prediction. It may be, as Schubert suggests, that "the power of any science lies in its capacity to make successful predictions." [5] But successful prediction alone is not what distinguishes scientific endeavor. Scholars and ordinary people are constantly making predictions — some with greater success than others.[6] The scientist seeks prediction based objectively on the measurement of relationships of observed data; to most people, and often to scientists as well, prediction is intuitive and based on less than complete data. It is this goal of more objectivity and increased reliability of prediction and inference which supplies the major motivation for much of the work described below.

II

Both historically and analytically, attempts to relate social backgrounds to judicial decisions have fallen into three distinct categories. The first, primarily descriptive, involves the systematic collection and organization of a variety of background data. Practically speaking, this means gathering such information about each judge in the sample as age, ethnic and religious affiliations, parental occupations, career patterns, prior judicial office, party affiliation, education, and so forth — the number of factors being limited only by the availability of data or the imagination of the researcher.

Studies of this kind date back to the 1930's, but the most recent and influential has been John Schmidhauser's "Collective Portrait" of the Justices of the Supreme Court.[7] Published in 1959, this

---

[5] Schubert, *Judicial Attitudes and Voting Behavior: The 1961 Term of the United States Supreme Court*, 28 LAW & CONTEMP. PROB. 100, 102 (1963). The goal of predictability for "reckoning" is also discussed in LLEWELLYN, THE COMMON LAW TRADITION — DECIDING APPEALS 11–18 (1960).

[6] Legal scholars frequently attempt to predict judicial actions. Fred Rodell correctly forecast the results and the votes of seven of eight justices participating in *Baker v. Carr*. Rodell, *For Every Justice, Judicial Deference is a Sometime Thing*, 50 GEO. L.J. 700 (1962).

[7] Schmidhauser, *The Justices of the Supreme Court: A Collective Portrait*, 3 MIDWEST J. OF POLITICAL SCIENCE 1 (1959). For examples of earlier studies see

study provided the most detailed analysis of the backgrounds of
the Justices ever assembled, served to demonstrate clearly the
upper middle class bias of judicial recruitment patterns, and
stimulated a host of similar inquiries. In addition to identifying
patterns of selections shedding considerable light on the judicial
selection process, such implications also provide the basis for
plausible, though unsystematic, inferences about the sorts of
values likely to dominate a court in a particular period.[8] Furthermore, such efforts illuminate one way in which power and status
are distributed among various groups and interests in society —
what Krislov has called the "representational question."[9]

The second category involves attempts to relate these background characteristics to actual decision patterns, measuring the
degree to which a particular characteristic is regularly associated
with a particular type of decision. Of the many studies in this
category, those by Nagel,[10] Schmidhauser,[11] Goldman,[12] Sprague,[13]
and Danelski[14] have been chosen for specific attention. Though
these studies differ somewhat in research design and results, all
share certain basic theoretical assumptions. First, they all accept
the "dynamic" view of the judicial function outlined in the first
section. Second, they all accept the utility — for research purposes — of abstracting a single item, or variable, from a complex process and treating it in isolation. This leads to what may
seem to be a contrary and overly simplistic view of the sources and
motivations of judicial behavior — almost akin to mechanical

EWING, THE JUDGES OF THE SUPREME COURT, 1789–1937: A STUDY OF THEIR
QUALIFICATIONS (1938); Mott, Albright & Semmerling, *Judicial Personnel,* 167
ANNALS OF THE AMERICAN ACADEMY OF POLITICAL AND SOCIAL SCIENCE 143 (1933).

[8] *Cf.* GROSSMAN, LAWYERS AND JUDGES — THE ABA AND THE POLITICS OF JUDI-
CIAL SELECTION 196–207 (1965).

[9] KRISLOV, THE SUPREME COURT IN THE POLITICAL PROCESS 30 (1965).

[10] Nagel, *Political Party Affiliation and Judges' Decisions,* 55 AM. POL. SCI.
REV. 843 (1961); *Testing Relations Between Judicial Characteristics and Judicial
Decision-Making,* 15 WESTERN POL. Q. 425 (1962); *Ethnic Affiliations and Judicial
Propensities,* 24 J. OF POLITICS 92 (1962); *Judicial Backgrounds and Criminal
Cases,* 53 J. CRIM. L., C. & P.S. 333 (1962).

[11] Schmidhauser, *Judicial Behavior and the Sectional Crisis of 1837–1860,* 23
J. OF POLITICS 615 (1961); *Stare Decisis, Dissent. and the Background of the
Justices of the Supreme Court of the United States,* 14 U. OF TORONTO L.J. 194
(1962).

[12] Goldman, Politics, Judges, and the Administration of Justice, unpublished
Ph.D. dissertation, Harvard University, 1965.

[13] Sprague, Voting Patterns on the United States Supreme Court: Cases in
Federalism, 1889–1959, unpublished Ph.D. dissertation, Stanford University, 1964.

[14] DANELSKI, A SUPREME COURT JUSTICE IS APPOINTED (1964).

jurisprudence. But all these scholars recognize — to differing degrees and in differing weights — the importance of institutional factors in accounting for particular decisions or groups of decisions. None suggests, except in the abstract, that any particular background variable "accounts" for certain types of decisions. All reject theories of causality which seem to establish a direct dependent relationship between a background variable and a line of cases. Rather, they argue that evidence of a highly significant statistical relationship [15] between a background variable and a decisional pattern is both relative and associational. For example, though all but Danelski treat political party affiliation as a major independent variable, none suggests that for a judge to have been a Republican or a Democrat automatically results in certain types of decisions. They do suggest that, when placed on a continuum, Democratic judges are more likely to vote in certain ways than Republican judges in certain types of cases. Finally, with the single exception of Danelski, all operate solely with aggregates of judges and cases; they are interested in generalized patterns of association, rather than in discrete individual actions.

These studies also share some methodological techniques. Regardless of the type or level of court being studied, unanimous decisions are eliminated from all samples. While this emphasis on intracourt division certainly introduces an element of bias, particularly since the majority of all cases are decided unanimously,[16] there is no way of including unanimous cases when *comparing* judges. The mere fact that most judges on most courts tend to agree most of the time tells us something about the common process of conditioning and socialization that they undergo and further serves to caution us against placing undue emphasis on the

---

[15] "Statistical significance" is a technical term, not to be confused with "importance" or "validity." To say that a finding is statistically significant at the ".05" level means that the finding would not have occurred by chance more than five times in a hundred. As a matter of convention, a finding which has a random probability of less than .05 is described as "statistically significant."

[16] Goldman found that the rate of division on the courts of appeals varied by circuit, from 2.8% to 15.5% over a three-year period. See Goldman, *supra* note 12, at 191. Unanimous decisions of the United States Supreme Court constitute a much smaller proportion of that Court's decisions. In all cases involving federalism questions from 1910 to 1959, the percentages of divided cases, by decades, were 15, 21, 26, 53, and 56. See Sprague, *supra* note 13, at 78. In the cases decided in its 1964 term the Supreme Court divided in 61.4% of its full opinion cases and 29.3% of its memorandum orders. See *The Supreme Court, 1964 Term,* 79 HARV. L. REV. 103, 109 (1965).

differences among them. But whatever correctives are needed can properly be postponed until we have adequately understood the reasons for patterns of division. In addition, all these authors assume, for purposes of analysis, a simplistic stimulus-response model of judicial behavior: the case is pictured as presenting a clear and uniform stimulus to all judges on a particular court, the judges' votes constitute the primary response, and the background characteristic being tested is the major intervening variable. In fact, of course, all of the judges hearing a particular case may perceive it differently, and their responses may be distillations of complex factors. But techniques of analysis are still too crude to permit the more refined models which would properly account for this complexity.

Nagel's study involved an analysis of the decisional propensities of a sample of the justices of the United States Supreme Court and state courts of last resort — the sample consisting of the 298 judges listed in the 1955 *Directory of American Judges* who were still serving at the close of 1955.[17] Limiting himself to those courts on which there was at least one member of each party, Nagel analyzed all the 1955 cases for each court in fifteen areas of law, determining decisional propensities for each court and decisional scores for each judge. Hypothetically, if the Ames Supreme Court decided 10 of 21 criminal cases for the defendant, and Judge A, a Republican, voted 3 times for the defendant, he would have a decisional score of 3/21 or .14, considerably below the court's mean defendant-support score of .48. If the decisional scores of Republicans on that court were generally in the .14–.40 range, while the scores of Democrats were in the .50–.80 range, Nagel would conclude that there was a strong and possibly significant relationship between party affiliation and propensity to decide for the defendant in criminal cases.[18]

Nagel's findings showed that "in all 15 types of cases the Democratic judges were above the average decision scores of their respective courts (in what might be considered a liberal direction) to a greater extent than the Republican judges."[19] Nagel found that Democratic judges were more prone to favor (1) the defense in criminal cases, (2) administrative agencies in business regula-

---

[17] Nagel, *Political Party Affiliation and Judges' Decisions*, 55 Am. Pol. Sci. Rev. 843 (1961).

[18] *Id.* at 845.

[19] *Ibid.*

tion cases, (3) the private party in cases involving regulation of nonbusiness entities, (4) the claimant in unemployment compensation cases, (5) the libertarian position in free speech cases, (6) the finding of a constitutional violation in criminal cases, (7) the government in tax cases, (8) the divorce seeker in divorce cases, (9) the wife in divorce settlement cases, (10) the tenant in landlord-tenant disputes, (11) the labor union in union-management cases, (12) the debtor in debt collection cases, (13) the consumer in sales of goods cases, (14) the injured party in motor vehicle accident cases, and (15) the employee in employee injury cases. Nine of these findings (1, 2, 4, 6, 7, 10, 13, 14, and 15) proved to be statistically significant relationships.

Nagel concluded that, in these areas of decision, Democratic judges were *more likely than* Republican judges to support the designated liberal position, a result consistent with the findings of Schubert,[20] Ulmer,[21] and Vines,[22] and, in part, with the findings of Goldman and Bowen reported below. Similar policy differences between Democrats and Republicans have been found to exist among Congressmen and the electorate.[23] Nagel did not suggest a "party-line" theory of judicial decision-making but rather that the same factors which resulted in party identification also resulted in more or less liberal decisions, with party affiliation operating as a "feedback reinforcement." [24] In parallel studies, Nagel found that judges who had been public prosecutors, members of the American Bar Association, or Protestants took the "Republican" position more often and were less likely to support the defendant in criminal cases than their brethren, findings which are clearly consis-

---

[20] Schubert found Democratic judges on the Michigan Supreme Court more favorably inclined towards workmen's compensation claims. SCHUBERT, QUANTITATIVE ANALYSIS OF JUDICIAL BEHAVIOR 129–42 (1959).

[21] Ulmer extended Schubert's analysis and concluded that "Democratic justice is more sensitive to the claims of the unemployed and the injured than Republican justice." Ulmer, *The Political Party Variable in the Michigan Supreme Court*, 11 J. PUB. L. 352, 362 (1962).

[22] Vines's study of the voting patterns of federal district judges in the South found consistently more Republicans among the "moderate" and "integrationist" blocs than among those judges most disposed to favor segregationist claims. Vines, *Federal District Judges and Race Relations Cases in the South*, 26 J. OF POLITICS 337, 350–51 (1964).

[23] See, *e.g.*, CAMPBELL, CONVERSE, MILLER & STOKES, THE AMERICAN VOTER 39–115 (1960); TRUMAN, THE CONGRESSIONAL PARTY (1959); McCloskey, Hoffman & O'Hara, *Issue Conflict and Consensus Among Party Leaders and Followers*, 54 AM. POL. SCI. REV. 406 (1960).

[24] Nagel, *supra* note 17, at 847.

tent with existing data on the backgrounds of identifiers with each party.[25]

Schmidhauser's studies focus exclusively on United States Supreme Court Justices. In one study, he examined the relationship of regional background to the decision in 52 major cases involving "sectional rivalry" between 1837 and 1860. Did the Justices "consistently split on regional lines despite other possibly compelling factors such as attitudes toward national supremacy, the integrity of the judicial institution, or the position of their political parties?"[26] Relying primarily on the technique of scalogram analysis, Schmidhauser was able to isolate regional divisions in the voting patterns and hypothesize that (1) among Justices who took extreme positions, party and sectional background both seemed to strengthen underlying attitudes toward regionally divisive issues, and (2) among moderate and neutral judges, party frequently proved stronger than regional background.

In a second study, Schmidhauser sought to test the *a priori* assertion that prior judicial experience was positively related to judicial restraint, particularly to a strong adherence to stare decisis. Focusing on the 81 decisions of the Supreme Court in which a valid precedent had been expressly overruled,[27] he established a "propensity to overrule" score for each Justice participating in one or more of these decisions and then compared these scores with the amount of prior experience each Justice had. The finding was that Justices with experience on lower courts had a greater propensity to abandon stare decisis than did Justices without such experience. While the data did not justify a conclusion of such an inverse relationship, it seemed at least to rebut opposite *a priori* assertions.[28] Schmidhauser also found that Justices who most frequently dissented were those with the lowest propensities to overrule, and he concluded from this and other data that contrary to

---

[25] Nagel, *Judicial Backgrounds and Criminal Cases*, 53 J. Crim. L., C. & P.S. 333, 335 (1962).

[26] Schmidhauser, *Judicial Behavior and the Sectional Crisis of 1837–1860*, 23 J. of Politics 615, 621, 627 (1961).

[27] Schmidhauser recognizes the vulnerability of this index as a true measure of "propensity to overrule," since it neglects the perhaps more revealing solo dissenting opinions in favor of abandoning precedent. Schmidhauser, *Stare Decisis, Dissent, and the Background of the Justices of the Supreme Court of the United States*, 14 U. of Toronto L.J. 194, 199 (1962).

[28] *Id.* at 202. Ulmer's finding of a positive relationship between experienced judges and court stability is in point here. Ulmer, *Homeostasis in the Supreme Court*, in Judicial Behavior 170 (Schubert ed. 1964).

a common impression, the typical dissenter was not a fire-breathing doctrinal innovator, but rather a "tenacious advocate of traditional doctrines which were being abandoned." [29]

Goldman's method was similar to that of Nagel and Schmidhauser, but his results can best be described as ambiguous. Goldman's sample included all nonunanimous cases decided by the United States courts of appeals from 1961 to 1964, a total of 2,510 cases and 2,776 issues.[30] After establishing liberal and conservative divisions within each court (panel), Goldman attempted to correlate the judges' scores with four sets of background variables — political, socio-economic, professional, and miscellaneous — such as age or ABA rating.[31] He found, like Nagel, that the Democratic judges had significantly higher liberalism scores in economic cases; but he found no differences between Democrats and Republicans in criminal cases or general civil liberties categories.[32] And he found that the marked differences Nagel noted between Catholic and Protestant judges — the former being more liberal — disappeared when party affiliation was controlled.[33] Part of the difference may have resulted from a different sample, since many of the judges Nagel studied were elected in partisan contests and were presumably more attuned to existing party ideologies.[34] Going beyond the party variable, Goldman's findings led him to conclude that "the background variables . . . tested . . . are not directly associated with uniform tendencies in judicial behavior." [35] Goldman does not discount background characteristics entirely as a generator and predictor of judicial behavior; but he is clearly skeptical of attributing any major significance to them.

Sprague's study of Supreme Court voting blocs in cases involving questions of federalism seems to reinforce Goldman's skep-

[29] Schmidhauser, *supra* note 27, at 209.

[30] The courts of appeals present a special problem because most cases are decided by rotating panels of three judges. Goldman's technique is specifically attuned to this problem. Goldman, *supra* note 12, at 46.

[31] The "ABA rating" mentioned is the preappointment evaluation of the judge by the Standing Committee on Federal Judiciary of the American Bar Association. See GROSSMAN, *op. cit. supra* note 8.

[32] Goldman, *supra* note 12, at 219.

[33] *Id.* at 237–41. Nagel's findings on religious affiliations were reported in *Ethnic Affiliations and Judicial Propensities*, 24 J. OF POLITICS 92 (1962).

[34] Nagel did, however, break down his sample into judges who were chosen in partisan or nonpartisan elections, finding no significant difference in the "party effect." Nagel, *supra* note 17, at 848.

[35] Goldman, *supra* note 12, at 254.

ticism. Unlike the aforementioned projects, Sprague's does not focus on individual judicial voting. His unit of analysis is the bloc, or group of Justices who tend to unite consistently in voting. Having established the existence of these blocs, Sprague sought to determine whether personal background characteristics "unambiguously discriminated" between the members of one bloc and those of other blocs. He found that the best discriminator was prior judicial experience, though none of the background variables was very adequate. In contrast to Nagel, he found that political party did not effectively discriminate between blocs except in the very limited area of property disputes.[36]

Danelski's study of Pierce Butler differs from the works already discussed in several ways. He deals only with a single Justice. And most important for analytical purposes, he has introduced an intermediate variable between the judge's background characteristics and his later behavior as a judge. From a total picture of Butler's early life and professional career, Danelski derives several key *values* which are then treated as independent variables. Butler is characterized as a "moralist, patriot, laissez-faire champion . . . . His was a world of . . . black or white, a world in which principle could never be sacrificed to expediency. He had a system of values for which he was willing to fight." [37]

Relating these values to Butler's work on the Supreme Court, Danelski finds significant areas of agreement or correlation, with the exception that Butler proved much more sensitive to procedural due process claims — in fact he was the "Court's champion of those claims from 1923 to 1939" — than his prior speeches and activities would have indicated. Danelski had "predicted," on the basis of a content analysis of Butler's speeches, that freedom, patriotism, and laissez-faire were his dominant substantive values, and adherence to stare decisis his dominant procedural value. All predictions in economic cases proved correct, while individual freedom, which probably accounted for Butler's record in due process cases, bowed to patriotism in free speech and internal security cases.[38]

---

[36] Sprague, *supra* note 13, at 144. The only attempt to test the impact of party affiliation at the trial court level has produced similarly negative results. Dolbeare, Trial Courts in the Political System: Policy Impact and Functions in an Urban Setting 177–83, 222–29, unpublished ms., University of Wisconsin, 1966.

[37] DANELSKI, *op. cit. supra* note 14, at 19.

[38] *Id.* at 180–99.

The picture which Danelski draws is that of a strong-willed judge who found support and encouragement for his personal values in the institutional life of the Court. But the question implicit in such a finding concerns the circumstances and conditions in which personal values derived from pre-judicial experiences are most likely to account for judicial decisions. None of the studies described so far has — or could have — gone further than to speculate about answers to such a question.

It is in attempting an answer to a related question that the third category of analysis becomes crucial. Assuming that statistically significant relationships between certain background characteristics and judicial behavior have been discovered, to what extent can these findings be said to account for the variance in judicial vote patterns? Quantitatively, inquiry can be made through the use of partial correlation coefficients and multiple regression analysis. Bowen's study of state and appellate judges is the only application so far of these techniques, and his findings are both encouraging and disturbing.[39] After replicating most of Nagel's and Schmidhauser's "associational" results,[40] Bowen found that none of the variables most significantly "associated" with judicial decisions explained more than a fraction of the total variance among judges. No single variable accounted for more than 16 per cent of the variance in any particular area, and most were in the 1 to 8 per cent range. With one exception, the combined explanatory power of the six variables tested never exceeded 30 per cent.[41] Even allowing for errors in sampling and measurement, Bowen's findings cast clear doubt on the explanatory power of background variables taken by themselves.[42] Mere tests of association are inadequate, though useful, and more powerful measures indicate

---

[39] Bowen, The Explanation of Judicial Voting Behavior from Sociological Characteristics of Judges, unpublished Ph.D. dissertation, Yale University, 1965. The partial correlation coefficient is a measure of the amount of the total variance explained by one independent variable when all other variables are controlled. Multiple regression analysis measures the amount of variance explained by all the independent variables together.

[40] On the basis of tests of association comparable to those used by Nagel, Bowen found party affiliation and age to be the most consistent independent variables. *Id.* at 187–89.

[41] *Id.* at 201.

[42] There is some problem with Bowen's data which detracts from his findings. His inclusion of unanimous cases may operate to depress the "amount of variance" explained. However, even if the amount of variance were doubled, it would seem that his essential pessimism is warranted.

the presence of other "intervening variables" between the case and the ultimate decision.

Bowen's study serves to emphasize Schmidhauser's warning: [43]

> It is not at all clear that the social and political background factors in themselves may serve as reliable indicators of precise patterns of judicial behavior. Explanations based entirely upon the causal influence of such factors . . . could scarcely take into account . . . the impact upon individual justices of the traditions of the Supreme Court itself or of the interaction of intelligent and frequently forceful personalities . . . . Complete dependence upon background factors would also ignore the complexity and subtlety of intellect and motivation . . . .

But his findings do not justify any inference that background variables are irrelevant. Rather, his results emphasize the importance of describing and analyzing the other intervening variables which interact with personal values, and of finding a way to integrate these variables in a theory which emphasizes their effect on judicial decisions.

III

Those who attempt to explain judicial behavior in terms of the backgrounds of the judges share with historians the problem of never knowing precisely how the past has influenced the present. But even allowing for these failings, background studies have made a contribution by systematically exploring an important dimension of judicial behavior. That early and crude efforts have not yet led to a perfect understanding of such behavior is surely not the measure of these efforts. Such a measure should weigh their contributions against present and potential results to be derived from other methods. A brief catalog of general contributions would include the identification of key background variables and some attempt at explaining their relationship to decisional patterns, the facility for handling quantities of data which extend the basis — in breadth and reliability — of inferences about the judicial process, and the ability to test conclusions and observations of traditional observers. Schmidhauser, for example, was able to demonstrate the shallowness of Rodell's claim that virtually

---

[43] SCHMIDHAUSER, THE SUPREME COURT: ITS POLITICS, PERSONALITIES AND PROCEDURES 57–58 (1960). For another view of these studies see BECKER, POLITICAL BEHAVIORALISM AND MODERN JURISPRUDENCE 31–36 (1964).

all of Chief Justice Taney's decisions could be "traced, directly or indirectly, to his big-plantation birth and background." [44] On the other hand, Danelski was able to demonstrate the substantial validity of contemporary observers' predictions that Butler's experience as a railroad lawyer would be clearly reflected in his Supreme Court votes on rate and valuation cases. [45] Danelski did not make the unwarranted generalization that all judges who had been railroad lawyers would have acted the same way as Butler; as Paul Freund has emphasized, the lawyer is not always father to the judge. [46] But an examination of all judges with "railroad" backgrounds might support such a generalization. Inferences and generalizations about the judicial process are all too often made on the basis of a very limited sample — the "great" cases or the work of the "great" judges — which ignore the run-of-the-mill business which constitutes the essence of the judicial process. No theory with any claim to significant explanatory power could afford to rely on such incomplete knowledge.

There is no doubt that preliminary attempts to isolate particular background variables have initially and necessarily overlooked the essentially cumulative and often random nature of human experience, as well as slighting the impact of institutional influences on the judicial mind. [47] That judges are (or were) Republicans or Catholics or corporate lawyers or law professors may tell everything about some judges. More likely it will tell only part of the story. Furthermore, not all judges can be easily classified as "liberal" or "conservative." Some categorization is inherent in all scholarship, but the demands of quantitative analysis in this regard may sometimes seem to be fulfilled at too great a cost. [48]

Finally, methods must be developed which measure judges' intensity of preference and which take into account the vast majority of decisions which are decided unanimously. The latter point is particularly crucial at this stage of research development, since it

---

[44] RODELL, NINE MEN 120 (1955).

[45] DANELSKI, *op. cit. supra* note 14, at 184–88.

[46] FREUND, THE SUPREME COURT OF THE UNITED STATES: ITS BUSINESS, PURPOSES AND PERFORMANCE 116 (1961).

[47] See, *e.g.*, Llewellyn's famous "Fourteen Points." LLEWELLYN, *op. cit. supra* note 5, at 19–61.

[48] Nagel's imputation of "liberalism" to supporting the "wife in divorce settlement cases" is an example of the possible arbitrariness in classifying cases, and Schmidhauser's finding on the basis of a single decision that Rufus Peckham had a "propensity to overrule" indicates the difficulty in classifying some behavior. See Nagel, *supra* note 27, at 200.

raises in peculiarly dramatic fashion the question of the actual impact of social backgrounds on judicial behavior. The hypothesis has been that backgrounds are a major cause of division or variance among the judges; but the contrary assumption, that background experiences contribute to consensus and unanimity, has never been carefully examined. In any case, what is required are further efforts in understanding the very subtle ways in which personal values derived from background experiences are articulated in the judical context.[49]

---

[49] See Goldman, *supra* note 12, at 20.

COURTS AS SMALL GROUPS

Walter F. Murphy *

COLLEGIAL courts and juries are small groups in a face-to-face relationship that interact under an obligation to solve a specific problem or set of problems. Reliable theories and perhaps even raw data about human behavior in small groups may thus be relevant to the study of the judicial process. This article will discuss the "state of the art" of small group sociology that may be useful to that study.

The initial problem is to define what is meant by a small group approach.[1] The studies clustered under the "small group" rubric have had many different orientations and objectives and have employed many different assumptions and data, but the focus of most of these investigations has been on collective decision-making.[2] This paper will refer to "a" small group approach rather than "the" approach, meaning research that puts a major emphasis on the processes of face-to-face interaction among members of the same group to produce a decision or a series of decisions.[3]

I

A major stimulus of small group studies of judicial behavior has been the work of C. Herman Pritchett of the University of Chicago. Beginning in the early 1940's Pritchett published a series of articles and *The Roosevelt Court*,[4] demonstrating the ex-

---

* Ford Research Professor of Governmental Affairs, Princeton University. A.B., Notre Dame, 1950; A.M., George Washington, 1954; Ph.D., Chicago, 1957.

[1] For discussion of the meaning of "small" and "group" and of related problems of a basic nature, see GOLEMBIEWSKI, THE SMALL GROUP chs. 2–3 (1962).

[2] For an introduction to the extensive small group literature see BASS, LEADERSHIP, PSYCHOLOGY, AND ORGANIZATIONAL BEHAVIOR (1960); HARE, BORGOTTA & BALES (eds.), SMALL GROUPS (1955).

[3] The definition thus excludes discussion of such interesting works as Ulmer, *Homeostatic Tendencies in the United States Supreme Court*, in INTRODUCTORY READINGS IN POLITICAL BEHAVIOR 168 (1961). For a summary of other useful definitions see VERBA, SMALL GROUPS AND POLITICAL BEHAVIOR 11–12 (1961).

[4] PRITCHETT, THE ROOSEVELT COURT (1948). This bloc analysis was extended on a more limited set of issues through the end of the Chief Justiceship of Fred Vinson in PRITCHETT, CIVIL LIBERTIES AND THE VINSON COURT (1954).

istence of cohesive voting blocs on the U.S. Supreme Court during the years 1937–1947. He relied in part on traditional case analysis but also used statistical analysis of the Justices' votes to show consistent tendencies of certain members of the Court to vote together on various classes of issues. The bloc analysis portion of his study depended entirely on the votes of the Justices.

In 1958 Eloise Snyder, a sociologist, published an analysis of the Supreme Court which considered whether the Court over a long time span (1921–1953) had divided into persistent subgroups, how changes in alignments occurred, and how new Justices found their position within the larger group.[5] Using as her data the votes of the Justices in all nonunanimous constitutional cases during the thirty-three year period, Snyder found that the Court divided into three subgroups: a liberal group, a conservative group, and a pivotal group that lacked a firm commitment. Snyder reported that these alignments were consistent. While a Justice might switch from a pivotal to a liberal or conservative sub-group or vice-versa, never did a Justice of the liberal sub-group cross over to the conservative bloc, and rarely did a Justice make the conservative-to-liberal transition without a pause in the pivotal group.[6] She noted a general tendency to shift to the right during a Justice's career but attributed this more to the Court moving to the left so as to make a Justice whose views did not change seem to shift to the right than to any change of views by the individual Justice. Newly appointed Justices tended to join the pivotal subgroup, the group that frequently held the balance of power. After a time on the Court they tended to gravitate to the right or left subgroup.

Since Pritchett and Snyder only used voting records they could discover little more than that Justices could be classified; study of groups also requires consideration of interpersonal interaction and influence. The fact that two or more Justices vote together is rather weak evidence that their votes are the result of interaction; standing alone, voting records tell very little about the force or direction of any interpersonal influence that may exist. Small group analysis requires other kinds of data and a more

---

[5] Snyder, *The Supreme Court as a Small Group*, 36 SOCIAL FORCES 232 (1958).

[6] Snyder was speaking in general terms; she did not mean that "liberals" and "conservatives" never voted together in individual cases. See also SCHUBERT, QUANTITATIVE ANALYSIS OF JUDICIAL BEHAVIOR 77–172 (1959); Loeb, *Judicial Blocs and Judicial Values in Civil Liberties Cases*, 14 AM. U.L. REV. 146 (1965).

general understanding of the impact of a group decisional situation on individual behavior.

Especially in the postwar period, social psychologists have produced a mass of literature on group decisional situations.[7] Their research was based on observation of people brought together under laboratory conditions and given a specific problem to solve. The experiments were designed to suggest and to test as rigorously as possible general hypotheses about leadership as a function of group interaction. Professor Robert Bales of Harvard, perhaps the leader in this field, developed a concept of the dual character of leadership: task leadership and social leadership.[8] The former seeks to complete the present task in the most effective and efficient manner; the latter seeks to provide the friendly atmosphere that eases cooperation. Experiments indicated that these two functions often are exercised by different persons within the group.

It is difficult to obtain direct observations of the judicial decision-making process. The private papers of deceased judges, however, constitute a fruitful source of information, and various judges have preserved their working papers — including intra-court memoranda, slip opinions as edited by colleagues, and occasionally notes taken during conference discussions — and arranged for their future use by scholars.

David Danelski, a lawyer and political scientist, was the first to utilize both the theoretical constructs of the small group sociologists and the information in judicial papers to apply a small group approach to a court.[9] Relying on materials found in the unpublished papers of a number of Justices, Danelski applied Bales' concept of dual leadership to the Supreme Court under Chief Justices Taft, Hughes, and Stone. Taft, he concluded, was the social leader of his court and relied on his close friend Willis Van Devanter to supply task leadership; Hughes exercised task leadership over his brethren and also offered some social leader-

---

[7] For an account of the historical development of this kind of analysis, see Faris, *Development of the Small-Group Research Movement*, in SHERIF & WILSON (eds.), GROUP RELATIONS AT THE CROSSROADS 155 (1953).

[8] BALES, INTERACTION PROCESS ANALYSIS (1950).

[9] Danelski, *The Influence of the Chief Justice in the Decisional Process*, in MURPHY & PRITCHETT (eds.), COURTS, JUDGES, AND POLITICS 497 (1961). Other scholars, of course, had used judicial papers, *e.g.*, MASON, HARLAN FISKE STONE (1956), but they did not use the tools developed by small group sociology. Those who criticize use of this kind of material are answered in LLEWELLYN, THE COMMON LAW TRADITION — DECIDING APPEALS 324 n.308 (1960).

ship; Stone played neither role and was unable to ally himself with one or more colleagues who could perform these functions.[10]

Danelski concluded that as a result of the comparative ability in social leadership, conflict among the Justices was more muted and cohesion more pronounced on the Taft Court than on the Hughes Court and far more so than on the Stone Court. Danelski ranks the Hughes Court somewhat ahead of that of Taft and well above that of Stone in terms of the effectiveness of task leadership — decisions produced in relation to conference time. Hughes's advantage in playing both roles was offset, Danelski believes, by Taft's greater skill as a social leader.

In a work related to Danelski's, I discussed how a Justice of the Supreme Court could lawfully act to maximize his influence on public policy development through a process of bargaining.[11] My objective was not to demonstrate how the judicial process typically operates but to explain the capability of a single Justice to affect the definition and allocation of values in our society. The Associate Justices of the U.S. Supreme Court are equal in authority, and the Chief Justice has only a small amount of additional authority. It may sometimes happen for a period of time, as with John Marshall, that a judge may by the power of his intellect and the sheer force of his personality lead his colleagues. Certainly one should not underestimate the importance in the judicial process of reasoned argument based on thorough research and grounded in deep learning, nor should one be willing without evidence to deny that even judges may be swayed by a great personality. Yet on many issues a Justice may find himself unable to convince colleagues even after massing all his erudition and dialectical skill, and even after emotional appeals. A Justice may thus find himself either: (a) with the majority on the result but

---

[10] Danelski's conclusion was based primarily on his analysis of the Stone papers in the Library of Congress and on the divisions within the Stone Court revealed in concurring and dissenting opinions. A later reading and partial analysis of the papers of Mr. Justice Frank Murphy at the University of Michigan indicate that Stone led the conference discussion at least to the extent of getting the other Justices to discuss the issues he thought crucial.

[11] MURPHY, ELEMENTS OF JUDICIAL STRATEGY ch. 3 (1964). My data consisted primarily of material drawn from Columbia University's Oral History Project, the papers of Presidents Coolidge, F. D. Roosevelt, and Truman, of Chief Justices Chase, Taft, Hughes, and Stone, and of Justices Lurton, McReynolds, Sutherland, and Murphy. Much of the analytical framework of this part of my study was built on the work of Danelski, Bales, and other small group sociologists, although I differed with them at several points.

unable to agree with other Justices on the reasoning to support the decision; (b) with the minority on both scores; or (c) with the majority on both points but faced with the publication of an acid dissent. In these situations he can strike out on his own and write his views just as he holds them, or he can negotiate with his colleagues and try to compromise existing differences.

Bickel and Wellington have criticized the Warren Court because some of its opinions appear to be "desperately negotiated documents," [12] but it would seem that many if not most opinions of the Court on major issues are negotiated documents.[13] I would also hypothesize that this kind of bargaining process occurs on any collegial court that follows similar formal procedures of group decision-making. If this is true, close reading of an opinion should include consideration of the compromises it may contain. What may seem inscrutable wisdom to the traditional case analyst may only be deliberate ambiguity designed to accommodate by its very vagueness conflicting doctrines. One would not expect nine or even five intelligent, individualistic, and strong-willed lawyers to agree readily on controversial and significant issues, much less on the doctrines to be established and reasoning to be used to justify any major ruling. As Justice Frankfurter observed after fourteen years on the bench: "When you have to have at least five people to agree on something, they can't have that comprehensive completeness of candor which is open to a single man, giving his own reasons untrammeled by what anybody else may do or not do if he put that out." [14] The bargaining and resulting compromise may be over trivial matters of literary style or over crucial doctrinal issues. The objects which a Justice has to trade are his vote and his concurrence in an opinion; his sanctions are his right to change his vote and his right to write a separate opinion. Quite clearly the effectiveness of the first sanction depends largely on the existing division within the Court and of the second on the Justice's literary skill and legal expertise. Bargaining may be the product of open negotiation or it may be accomplished tacitly. Brandeis, Bickel shows, was a master of the latter technique. Often he

---

[12] Bickel & Wellington, *Legislative Purpose and the Judicial Process: The Lincoln Mills Case*, 71 HARV. L. REV. 1, 3 (1957).

[13] See, *e.g.*, Mr. Justice Frankfurter's discussion of Justice Holmes's compromises in The Pipe Line Cases, 234 U.S. 548 (1914), FELIX FRANKFURTER REMINISCES 294–301 (Philips ed. 1960).

[14] *Id.* at 298.

would circulate a dissent within the Court, then withdraw it when the conservative majority modified the opinion of the Court.[15]

II

As I indicated in the opening paragraph of this paper, a small group approach offers no magic key to understanding judicial behavior.[16] One has to keep in mind, first, that social scientists have so far only a variety of hypotheses about behavior in small groups, most of which have been tested only in experimental, laboratory situations. Clearly one must not uncritically apply to the actions of professional judges concepts derived from the behavior of *ad hoc* groups assembled in a laboratory for the purpose of solving only one problem. The findings of small group sociologists should be treated only as working hypotheses until tested outside the laboratory. And of course no social scientist claims that the group environment is the only factor governing behavior. Small group analysis, as Golembiewski points out,[17] merely supplements understanding of individual psychology and of social forces operating in the larger social environment.

More specifically I have reservations about the orientation of much of the small group literature toward leadership. Stressing leadership as a product of a social situation may leave the impression that because the functions of leadership are needed, they will be performed. But a leadership void may exist and persist, or only be partially filled. Moreover, just as one must be careful not to mistake formal trappings for real leadership, so too one has to be careful not to equate role-playing with effective role-playing. For instance, though Hughes was able to center discussion on the questions he thought important and to conduct that discussion rapidly and efficiently, and though he soothed ruffled feelings and maintained a working level of harmony among the brethren, the vital question remains: having led them to be social and having led them through their tasks, was he able to lead the Justices to vote and to write opinions the way he wanted?[18] The inability of small group theories to provide answers or even a framework

---

[15] BICKEL, THE UNPUBLISHED OPINIONS OF MR. JUSTICE BRANDEIS 205–10 (1957).

[16] For perceptive general critiques of small group analysis, see GOLEMBIEWSKI, *op. cit. supra* note 1, and VERBA, *op. cit. supra* note 3.

[17] *Op. cit. supra* note 1, at 17.

[18] *Cf.* note 10 *supra*.

for answers to this question detracts from their usefulness; but it would not appear that the future establishment of such a framework is impossible.

A second set of difficulties with any small group approach involves available data. As already indicated, although voting records are important indicia of group interaction, they are of limited use. Direct observation is probably impossible to obtain. Interviews, however, might be of some help in filling the gaps, if the interviewer makes certain he stays away from issues that are or are likely soon to be *sub judice*.

The private papers of the Justices are extremely valuable here. They often reveal much about the force and direction of interpersonal influence and group interaction, yet they too are subject to limitations. Even where a Justice took and kept notes of conference discussion, as Murphy and Lurton did, the record is rarely complete and may suffer because of memory lapse and human bias. Further, since no Justice is apt to allow his papers to be used during his own lifetime, there will always be a time lag before they can be utilized.

Even with these difficulties, there are still advantages to a small group approach. Careful attention to assumptions and critical use of unproved hypotheses can avoid most of the theoretical pitfalls. And new research techniques can be invented to reduce problems with data.[19] It might even be worthwhile to try to simulate a court much as the Chicago project has done with juries. The simulation could be made part of an advanced course.[20]

Simulation employing students seems, however, better adapted to teaching participants about the nature of group decision-making than it is a promising research device. Nevertheless interaction among the students may suggest some useful ideas that can be tested in other ways. Another kind of panel might be composed of experts, perhaps lawyers with considerable experience in appellate advocacy, law professors, or former judges. This kind of

[19] See Ulmer, *Leadership in the Michigan Supreme Court*, in SCHUBERT (ed.), JUDICIAL DECISION-MAKING 13 (1963), which applies an imaginative series of methods based on concurrence in opinions.

[20] In a graduate seminar on the judicial process I have required students at one three-hour session to sit as a court, hear oral argument on a hypothetical dispute in constitutional law and then meet in conference to discuss and decide the case. After the conference the chief justice has assigned the opinion of the court. While allowing dissenting and concurring opinions, I coerced the majority into agreeing on an institutional opinion by giving each the same grade for the court's opinion.

simulation would probably be a more accurate research tool. The NAACP has on occasion utilized a similar procedure to prepare presentations before the Supreme Court.[21]

III

Although it may not be of any immediate use in winning a particular lawsuit, small group analysis has already done much to increase understanding — by social scientists as well as lawyers — of the judicial process; and the various approaches have not yet been nearly fully exploited. There have been few investigations of tribunals other than the U.S. Supreme Court.[22] It would be very useful to have comparative studies of the influence of the group situation in courts that follow other kinds of formal decisional procedures.[23] What difference does it make, for instance, that in some states the task of writing the opinion of the court is assigned on a strictly rotational basis? Or if, as in England and Canada, there is a tradition of seriatim rather than institutional opinions? Or if, as in civil law countries, there is a rule against separate opinions? Do any of these formal practices affect the exercise of leadership and bargaining among the judges? What kinds of informal rules or customs develop to protect the integrity of the court and maintain harmony between the majority and the minority? Most important, what effect do these formal and informal procedures have on the course of the development of law and public policy?[24]

---

[21] VOSE, CAUCASIANS ONLY 199–200 (1959).

[22] *But see* Sickels, *The Illusion of Judicial Consensus*, 59 AM. POL. SCI. REV. 100 (1965); Ulmer, *supra* note 3.

[23] For descriptions of the formal procedures allowed in various American courts see New York University Institute of Judicial Administration, Appellate Courts: International Operating Procedures, Preliminary Report (mimeo., 1957).

[24] For another view of the utility of small group analysis, see BECKER, POLITICAL BEHAVIORALISM AND MODERN JURISPRUDENCE 26–31 (1964).

THEORETICAL ATTEMPTS AT PREDICTING JUDICIAL BEHAVIOR

Samuel Krislov *

TWO general strategies are available for creating a field study based on scientific principle. One may start by the accumulation of data and build, straw by straw. Alternatively one can start with rigorously developed theoretical systems and thereafter use data to test the theorems. Both methods have been used successfully in the social sciences. Economics has evolved by deduction from logical methods and psychology from the accumulation of experimental data. However, both have progressed also through the use of the alternative methods. Until recent years the data-oriented approach has been more prevalent in political science than the theoretical route. The theoretical approach has been described quite well by William Riker: [1]

> The essential feature of this method is the creation of a theoretical construct that is a somewhat simplified version of what the real world to be described is believed to be like. This simplified version or model is a set of axioms (more or less justifiable intuitively) from which nonobvious general sentences can be deduced. These deduced propositions, when verified, become both an addition to the model and a description of nature. As more and more sentences are deduced and verified, greater and greater confidence in the validity of the axioms is felt to be justified. Conversely, the deduction of false or inconsistent sentences tends to discredit the axioms.

In practice, a field seems to progress as — and if — it moves from theory to empirical data and back to theory. Lawyers familiar with Cardozo's writings are no doubt aware that Tycho Brahe had to scan the skies painstakingly to lay the foundations for Copernicus.[2] But we are also informed by historians of science that Copernicus made leaps of speculative inference that no data available at the time justified.

---

* Associate Professor of Political Science, University of Minnesota. B.A., New York University, 1951, M.A., 1952; Ph.D., Princeton, 1955.

[1] RIKER, THE THEORY OF POLITICAL COALITIONS 7 (1962).

[2] CARDOZO, SELECTED WRITINGS 1 (Hall ed. 1947).

Given this situation it is very difficult to be dogmatic about which research strategy is better; the accumulation of data in the hope of theory, or the proliferation of theory with the expectation that data will limit, sharpen, improve, test, and in the most rigorous sense of the word "prove" the theories. It is particularly hard to be dogmatic in the behavioral sciences, for the advances have not been overly impressive in the light of the effort. Yet sufficient progress has been made to cause social scientists to persist in perhaps foolish dreams.

Scientists value prediction for its ability to demonstrate and test the general utility of a theory, particularly to disprove the theory if a logically-necessary prediction does not result. The general public looks on prediction as a demonstration of magical powers when it is successful.

However, it is understanding in its broadest sense, not merely prediction, that is sought. A useful distinction is made between "prediction" and "forecasting." [3] The scientist makes predictions; that is, he states that if certain conditions prevail, certain results will follow. Useful assumptions permit one to forecast actual behavior within limits. Understanding permits one to know what range of variation can be expected in the physical world and this often satisfies any reasonable purpose. But even though engineers allow a safety factor of 100 per cent, bridges do fall down. In short, prediction may coincide with forecasting where the precise conditions required in the prediction are met in real life or when the range of possibilities interpreted by the prediction clearly indicates outcomes sufficient for forecasting purposes as well.

Without the control over external events or the ability to manipulate variables, however, the social scientist is not often able to make what amounts to better than an informed forecast or an interpretive presentation of materials. In this sense, then, Karl Llewellyn was essentially correct as usual when he wrote that:[4]

> The lawyer does not ask: How does an appellate tribunal arrive at *a* decision, *some* decision, *any* decision — in general, as an approximative pattern, in perhaps three, even four or seven, cases out of ten? The lawyer asks, instead: How does *this* appellate tribunal

---

[3] Sibley, *The Limitations of Behavioralism*, in American Academy of Political and Social Sciences, The Limits of Behavioralism in Political Science 68, 83–86 (Oct. 1962).

[4] Llewellyn, The Common Law Tradition — Deciding Appeals 15–16 (1960).

arrive at *the particular and concrete answer* which it reaches *in the particular and concrete case?*

I know of no man in the social disciplines who would dare to ask such a question. . . . In the present state of the other social disciplines or of behavioral science at large — so far as published work goes — this would be a dream-inquiry. It would be fantastic.

The exceptions to this observation have not been successes.

II

A number of predictive models have been put forward in recent years which might suggest the realities of judicial decision. In the first instance a number of "frames of reference" or approaches to decision-making have been suggested in other realms of discourse, which presumably might have application to the judicial decision. Again Llewellyn's description is generally accurate:[5]

When the psychologists began to look into how people go about reaching decisions, the question they were concerned with was: how do people get to a decision at all, to any decision, when faced with a problem-situation out of life? Roughly, they arrived at the conclusion that if it was a true problem-situation, i.e., if it was really a puzzler, then it was seldom that the actual deciding was done by way of formal and accurate deduction in the manner of formal logic. The common process was rather one either of sudden intuition — a leap to some result that eased the tension; or else it was one of successive mental experiments as imagination developed and passed in review various possibilities until one or more turned up which had appeal.

In addition to concrete psychological studies of actual decisions, the work of Herbert Simon and Chester Barnard in public administration has dealt with the rationality of decision and the premises that would enter into a so-called rational decision. Simon has had second thoughts, however, and has decided that "rationality" — that is, the systematic sifting of all possible alternatives in the real world — is not even theoretically a mode or stance that would make sense to the decision-maker. Recent discussions have emphasized that "information costs" would overburden the decision-maker under these circumstances, and Simon has written of the "satisfying" decision which involves the

---

[5] *Id.* at 11.

definition of a satisfactory solution on the part of the decision-maker, or the scanning of a relatively limited class of possible decisions (presumably selected because intuition or experience suggests that the class probably contains the optimal decision), and the choosing of the most satisfactory possibility from among this limited class. Charles Lindblom has furthered this approach, partly in criticism of and partly along the same lines as Simon, in discussing "incremental" change as a mode of decision-making.[6]

The interest group approach to political science associated with the name of A. F. Bentley can be reformulated into a rationally deductive model with presumed predictive power. It is postulated that political decisions, including judicial decisions, result from political pressure exerted by opposing social forces. Groups are able to mobilize resources and bring them to bear upon decision structures. These groupings are not merely the organized pressure groups that we discuss so often; indeed, organizational groups are merely the top of the iceberg and an unimportant top at that. The hydraulic pressure of the operative sources, not always visible, determines outcomes. Should the decision not accord with the forces that truly operate in society an unstable situation results which eventually forces new decisions. (Thus, for example, Bentley anticipated correctly that *Paul v. Virginia* would be reversed; there was, however, a slight delay of some forty years in achieving this reversal which somewhat tarnishes the impressiveness of the forecast.)[7] Unfortunately, Bentley's almost pathological refusal to define his terms and to indicate precisely what constituted "interest" further limits the usefulness of the approach, and his hope that he had begun to "fashion a tool" has been belied by future experience. Neither Bentleyan interest analysis nor that of Roscoe Pound and his followers nor any other has proven to be anything like a precise predictor or measurer of events or even processes.

Llewellyn and Peltason illustrate, however, the importance of the "interest group" approach, both in assessing fundamental influences and in sensitizing observers to the existence and limits

---

[6] See, *e.g.*, MARCH & SIMON, ORGANIZATIONS (1959); LINDBLOM, THE INTELLIGENCE OF DEMOCRACY (1965). Martin Shapiro has applied Lindblom's analysis to the judicial process in *Stability and Change in Judicial Decision-Making: Incrementalism or Stare Decisis?*, 2 LAW IN TRANSITION QUARTERLY 134 (1965).

[7] Paul v. Virginia, 75 U.S. (8 Wall.) 168 (1868), was overruled by United States v. South-Eastern Underwriters Association, 322 U.S. 533 (1944). See BENTLEY, THE PROCESS OF GOVERNMENT 391–92 (1908).

of forces at play in judicial decision-making. These two men — and such writers as Clement Vose who derived their essential insights from projections of the group approach — have moved "realistic" accounts of decision processes from the level of lawyers' gossip to systematically described fact.[8]

Perhaps still the most fashionable theoretical approach in the social sciences remains "structural functionalism," particularly those versions associated with the writing of Talcott Parsons. Structural functionalism, however, suffers from even greater diffuseness than the interest group approach; it results typically in plausible possible explanations being put forward in the name of causality, where alternative interpretation could just as plausibly be put forward. In the judicial area it has been followed in a few attempts that principally use new nomenclature for familiar facts. For example, little of moment results from referring to the Department of Justice as a "subsystem."[9]

The most widely utilized and most promising models of behavior are to be found in the class of formulations known as "game theory." The name has been both fortunate and unfortunate for the development of the approach, for the term itself has a certain surface attractiveness but also detracts from the seriousness of the endeavor. The approach has a long history in past mathematical formulations but gained curency as a result of the greater precision given to it by John Von Neumann, a famous mathematician, physicist, and developer of modern computer technology. This almost legendary figure combined his interest in poker with a genuine mathematical desire to formulate rules for the discovery of rational strategies in specific game situations. Together with Oskar Morgenstern, he found application for his general approach in economic and business behavior [10] — with considerable implications, for example, for business location and nature and extent of inventories — and others have found his formulations useful in discovering military strategy. The basic proposition of game theory is that, under certain conditions, a "pure strategy" exists which will guarantee a minimum return no matter what the op-

---

[8] See generally LLEWELLYN, *op. cit. supra* note 4; PELTASON, FIFTY-EIGHT LONELY MEN (1961); VOSE, CAUCASIANS ONLY (1959).

[9] See, *e.g.*, SCHUBERT, JUDICIAL POLICY-MAKING (1965). See also Herndon, *The Role of the Judiciary in State Political Systems*, in JUDICIAL BEHAVIOR 153 (Schubert ed. 1964).

[10] See generally VON NEUMANN & MORGENSTERN, THEORY OF GAMES AND ECONOMIC BEHAVIOR (3d ed. 1953).

ponent's behavior and will augment the payoff should the opponent behave in an irrational fashion.

In the field of international relations both rigorous and looser models based upon "game theory" approaches have been utilized as guidelines for decision behavior and general orientation of decision-makers. Thomas Schelling has explicitly argued the case for looser and more realistic applications of game theory. Herman Kahn has moved in similar directions. In the field of judicial behavior many of the relatively less precise, yet highly suggestive works on strategy, especially the work of Walter Murphy, have taken the same approach.[11]

It is obvious that collegial courts must arrive at a final opinion through an interactional process of discussion in bargaining. But that process remains largely undescribed and unexplored, presumably because of the difficulties of research. In *The Common Law Tradition*, Llewellyn suggested that a lawyer could gain a sense of continuity in law principally by "reading the bench" and learning to anticipate the responses of specific judges. Presumably this is possible so long as continuity prevails within a panel. But what range of change might one anticipate from the arrival of new personnel? What mix of decision can one anticipate in courts of appeals with a variety of combinations of panels possible?

The development of notions of influence and interaction as a matter of continuity together with shrewd observation should result in the formulation of general rules and combinations which could yield expectations on interactions. Murphy's *Elements of Judicial Strategy* [12] is perhaps more successful as an historical inquiry into specified events on the Supreme Court than it is as a genuine synthesis of existing theory on judicial or other types of decision-making. But it does establish the historical record that discrete individuals thrown together interact somewhat differently conjointly than they would in remote and indirect fashion. As in many other areas the whole is different from the parts. Marshall's record in assimilating into his own sphere of influence successive Jeffersonian appointees is only the most famous illustration and confirmation of that proposition. Murphy's

---

[11] See generally SCHELLING, THE STRATEGY OF CONFLICT (1960) ; Kahn, *Strategy, Foreign Policy, and Thermonuclear War*, in AMERICA ARMED 43 (Goldwin ed. 1963).

[12] MURPHY, ELEMENTS OF JUDICIAL STRATEGY (1964).

pioneering attempt provides material for more systematic treatment and more rigorous theorization. Informed by theory, he has presented cogent illustrations which in turn could be utilized to study other outcomes. Less ambitious but more rigorous attempts to apply theoretical models have also been essayed. Schubert, for example, has utilized stricter game theory formulations in his studies of FELA voting. He has suggested that the Justices consciously adopt a "pro-workmen" or "anti-workmen" strategy in voting on certiorari petitions and on the merits, and that the optimum strategy suggested by game theory is closely approximated by actual behavior. Schubert shows that by playing a "pure strategy," a bloc of Justices can use the decision on whether to grant certiorari in order to maximize the proportion of favorable results in those cases in which certiorari is granted.[13] However, Walter Berns has shown Schubert's analysis to be overly subtle, in having overlooked a more direct strategy with greater payoffs — simply voting according to a desired outcome in such cases.[14]

By being more restrictive and therefore less "true to life in assumptions" one can rigorously project expected strategies which could be conducive toward the accomplishment of aims and compare them with observed behavior of judges. In his *Quantitative Analysis of Judicial Behavior*,[15] Schubert applied game theory to an analysis of voting patterns on the Hughes Court, seeking particularly to understand the voting patterns and motivation of Chief Justice Hughes and Justice Roberts. He assumed that the objective of Hughes and Roberts (described as the hypothetical composite personality "Hughberts") was the desire to control decisions, to act as the pivot or fulcrum unit of the Court. Utilizing a specific application of game theory, the Shaply-Schubick index for determining power, which is defined precisely in terms of just such attainment of the pivotal position, Schubert found "Hughberts" had indeed acted in close correspondence with such predicted behavior, with the expected payoffs. Of course this confrontation by itself does no more than suggest the possibility of such motivation. In any event the suggestion that Roberts and

---

[13] Schubert, *The Certiorari Game*, in JUDICIAL BEHAVIOR 415–42 (Schubert ed. 1964).

[14] Berns, *Law and Behavioral Science*, 28 LAW AND CONTEMP. PROB. 185, 189–91 (1963).

[15] SCHUBERT, QUANTITATIVE ANALYSIS OF JUDICIAL BEHAVIOR 192–210 (1959).

Hughes behaved in that fashion is hardly new, and the belief that their behavior was power-oriented is at least as old as Irving Brant's "How Liberal is Justice Hughes?" [16]

In similar fashion, one may deduce the logical possibilities in the dynamism of numbers and the consequent effect upon affiliation of individuals as different patterns of coalitions emerge within the Supreme Court, if one makes the assumption that merely being determinative is the primary motive. Such deductions coincide fairly closely with what has been observed previously in such bodies. It can be shown that the difference between, say, three votes and four votes in such a body is more crucial than the mere additive value of one-ninth of the strength of the Court. Additionally, it can be demonstrated that the strength of a coalition depends not only upon its own vote but in part upon the total pattern of distribution within the body. (For example, a two-man coalition shares power equally with the other factions when the distribution of the remaining votes is four to three but has no influence if there is a durable coalition that has five or six votes within it.) Crucial occasions in voting distributions can and do occur where the change of one or two votes radically upsets the total balance upon the Court.[17]

It would be foolish, of course, to assume that in a real sense "power" — the securing of a decisive position which is itself an artificial definition of power — represents the totality of any sane judge's motives. General views of justice and the judicial role, the relation of the Court's position to other agencies in the governmental structure, to say nothing of the facts of the case, all play a fundamental role in determining actual votes and outcomes.

But economic motives are not truly the totality of influences on even the average poker player. Indeed, except for a tiny minority who manage consistently to accumulate large winnings, the mere presence of an individual at the game is prima facie evidence of other motivations, since the time spent could be utilized for far greater pecuniary gain in alternative fields of profitable endeavor. Nonetheless, most of the actions within the game can

---

[16] Brant, *How Liberal is Justice Hughes?*, New Republic, July 21, 1937, p. 295.

[17] Schubert, *The Power of Organized Minorities in a Small Group*, 9 ADMINISTRATIVE SCIENCE Q. 133 (1964); Krislov, *Power and Coalition in a Nine-Man Body*, Am. Behavioral Scientist, April 1963, p. 24.

best be understood if the expectation of reward is seen as the "true" goal of the players — though we always know better.

In the same way social scientists seek simplifying concepts. They assume that later complications of these notions can indeed be advanced if not to provide an explanation directly, then, at a minimum, to provide a base line or measuring point indicating deviations from some sort of predicted behavior. For example, Ulmer has followed the suggestion of "power" as the key desideratum among Justices with a demonstration of the fact that voting coalitions have not in fact been sufficiently durable to suggest bloc voting for that purpose alone.[18] He suggests that the behavior of the Justices fits better the expected patterns which would occur because of ideological affinities. (However, he has no formulas which would suggest what such behavior on the basis of ideological affinity would look like.) Blind adherence to a dominant value of achieving minimum sized coalitions is not the rule on the Court, as any experienced observer would have conceded from the beginning.

It is possible to complicate the notion of accumulation of minimum coalitions with less restrictive formulations which include the concept of "preferred coalitions" or ideological affinities. Applications of the coalition formulas developed in accordance with both expectations of power and tendencies toward favored coalitions on the part of the participants would seem to be a follow-up step in connection with the judicial process.[19]

As the present sketch of the state of deductions from former models indicates — though this sketch is by no means exhaustive — this style of research has not been popular with regard to judicial decision-making; more emphasis has been placed upon "attitudes" and "values" as components of the decision — presumably for the *post hoc* reasons only very recently urged by Schubert:[20]

> We expect, therefore, that prediction will be most likely to succeed between adjacent classes of variables: between cultural and attribute variables; between attribute and either cultural or atti-

---

[18] Ulmer, *Toward a Theory of Sub-Group Formation in the United States Supreme Court*, 27 JOURNAL OF POLITICS 133 (1965).

[19] LUCE & RAIFFA, GAMES AND DECISIONS 163 (1957); Gamson, *An Experimental Test of a Theory of Coalition*, in STEINER & FISHBEIN, CURRENT STUDIES IN SOCIAL PSYCHOLOGY 396 (1965).

[20] SCHUBERT, JUDICIAL POLICY-MAKING 123 (1965).

tudinal variables; between attitudinal and either attribute or decisional variables; and between decisional and attitudinal variables. This implies that the prediction of judicial decision-making behavior will be most successful if it is based upon the observation and measurement of judicial attitudes.

But proximity, time, and logic do not necessarily result in the discovery of causality, and indeed often result in a casuistic restatement of the problem in other language.

In view of current revival of interest in more formal models — along the line of the economic theorists — for the study of political parties, governmental and economic policy determination, and legislative behavior, it appears likely that the spread of theoretical efforts will continue to make itself felt in the judicial field as well.

THE CUMULATIVE SCALING OF JUDICIAL DECISIONS

Joseph Tanenhaus *

W HAT moves an appellate judge to decide a case as he does? To this time-honored query behavioralists are apt to reply that the judge's structure of social, economic, and political values is perhaps the most important single factor. His value structure leads to judicial attitudes, to predispositions toward deciding given types of cases in particular ways. A judge may, for example, be predisposed to support — or to deny — legal claims by labor unions, criminal defendants, racial minorities, federal regulatory agencies, or state and local authorities. If their assumptions are correct, behavioralists should be able to develop methods to identify the judicial attitudes held by various members of the bench — to explain why individual judges decided particular cases in the past, even in the absence of written opinions, and also to predict how these judges will act in the future.

One of the methods employed by some leading behavioralists to determine the attitudes judges hold and the extent to which these attitudes can account for their decisions is commonly referred to as cumulative scaling.[1] Other terms frequently used to describe this analytical tool are "scalogram analysis" and "Guttman scaling." In this essay three principal tasks have been set: (1) to explain what cumulative scaling is; (2) to indicate the potential utility of cumulative scaling; and (3) to evaluate major efforts to construct such scales.

---

* Professor of Political Science, University of Iowa. A.B., Cornell, 1947, A.M., 1949, Ph.D., 1953.
[1] Four persons in particular have devoted substantial attention to cumulative scaling: John R. Schmidhauser, Glendon Schubert, Harold J. Spaeth, and S. Sidney Ulmer. See, *e.g.*, SCHMIDHAUSER, CONSTITUTIONAL LAW IN THE POLITICAL PROCESS 486 (1963) ; SCHUBERT, THE JUDICIAL MIND (1965) ; Spaeth, *Unidimensionality and Item Variance in Judicial Scaling*, 10 BEHAVIORAL SCIENCE 290 (1965) ; Ulmer, *The Political Party Variable in the Michigan Supreme Court*, 11 J. PUB. L. 352 (1962) ; Ulmer, *Scaling Judicial Cases: A Methodological Note*, Am. Behavioral Scientist, April 1961, p. 31. See also the exchange of communications between Ulmer and Tanenhaus in 55 AM. POL. SCI. REV. 599 (1961).

I. WHAT CUMULATIVE SCALING IS

The initial objective in cumulative scaling is to determine whether a set of phenomena such as the votes cast by the members of a court in a group of cases can be arranged in an ordinal relationship. The requirements and implications of this process can be most readily grasped if preliminary attention is directed to three clearly distinguishable scales of measurement: nominal scales, ordinal scales, and interval scales.[2]

(a) *Nominal scales.* — A nominal scale requires only that objects be assigned to classes with regard to a given characteristic. Civil liberties issues furnish an example. Either a case contains a civil liberties issue or it does not. The relationship among all cases in a given class is one of identity and the relationship between classes that of nonidentity. Since *Korematsu v. United States* (sustaining the wartime Japanese evacuation) and *Martin v. City of Struthers* (invalidating a city ordinance which barred door-to-door distribution of religious literature) both contain a civil liberties issue, nominal scaling assumes that *Korematsu* equals *Struthers*, that *Struthers* equals *Korematsu*, and that each is equal to any other case containing a civil liberties issue. One cannot say that *Korematsu* contains a more or less important civil liberties issue than *Struthers* or *Brown v. Board of Education* (invalidating racial segregation in public schools), or *Murdock v. Pennsylvania* (invalidating a municipal license tax as applied to religious colporteurs).[3]

Nominal scales are the most primitive and the least powerful level of measurement. In fact, many scholars deny that they involve measurement in any meaningful sense at all. But, of course, this is merely a matter of definition. Strictly speaking only very limited types of statistics may be appropriately used with data that are nominally scaled. These include class modes, frequencies, and contingency correlations between classes. To be sure, recent developments in nonparametric statistics make it easier to test some kinds of hypotheses about judicial behavior which

---

[2] For an elementary discussion see SELLTIZ, JAHODA, DEUTSCH & COOK, RESEARCH METHODS IN SOCIAL RELATIONS 186–97 (rev. ed. 1959). For a more advanced treatment see TORGERSON, THEORY AND METHODS OF SCALING 1–40 (1958).

[3] Korematsu v. United States, 323 U.S. 214 (1944); Martin v. City of Struthers, 319 U.S. 141 (1943); Brown v. Board of Educ., 347 U.S. 483 (1954); Murdock v. Pennsylvania, 319 U.S. 105 (1943).

have been classified via nominal scaling — *if, and only if, certain additional assumptions are made.*[4]

(*b*) *Ordinal scales.* — To be positioned on an ordinal scale, objects must, as with nominal measurement, share the basis for classification with every other object in the class. But in addition it is necessary to be able to specify whether each object (or sub-class of objects) so classified is equal to (=), greater than (>), or less than (<) every other object (or sub-class) in the class. Returning to the Supreme Court decisions referred to above, let us suppose that *Brown* contains a more important civil liberties issue than *Korematsu* (B > K), *Korematsu* a more important civil liberties issue than *Struthers* (K > S), and *Struthers* a civil liberties issue equal in importance to that in *Murdock* (S = M). Then it must follow that B > S, B > M, K > M, M < B, M < K, S < B, and M = S. Technically the relationship between un-equal objects is transitive and asymmetrical, while the relation-ship between equal objects is transitive and symmetrical. Even more than in the case of nominal scales, a useful array of appro-priate nonparametric statistics has been developed.[5]

Most attitude and ranking scales aspire to reach at least this level of measurement. Only medians, percentiles (but not per-centages or means), and statistics based upon them are isomorphic to ordinal scaling and so appropriate for use with data so scaled. In other words, if we use means, standard deviations, and the like with ordinally scaled data, we do not satisfy the assumptions required by the models upon which these statistics are based.

(*c*) *Interval scales.* — With the interval scale a level of meas-urement is attained which is quantitative in the ordinary sense of the term. The objects (or sub-classes) in a class must, as in nominal measurement, share a given characteristic, and, as in ordinal measurement, they must be subject to ranking in accord with it. In addition, the distances, or intervals, between objects must bear the same relationships as intervals do in a numeric system. Not only is 5 < 10 < 15, but the interval between 5 and 10 is equivalent to the interval between 10 and 15. This does not imply (as does the structure of cardinal numbers) that 10 is twice

---

[4] Numerous illustrations of their uses and a discussion of the assumptions re-quired appear in Tanenhaus, *Supreme Court Attitudes Toward Federal Adminis-trative Agencies, 1947–1956 — An Application of Social Science Methods to the Study of the Judicial Process,* 14 VAND. L. REV. 473 (1961).

[5] For a useful introduction to nonparametrics, see SIEGAL, NONPARAMETRIC STATISTICS FOR THE BEHAVIORAL SCIENCES (1956).

and 15 three times as large as 5. An absolute zero point would be necessary if this were to be the case. Nevertheless, most of the more powerful standard statistics, means, standard deviations, correlation, regression, variance, and factor analytic techniques are generally appropriate for use with data that form interval scales because these satisfy the assumptions required by the models upon which the statistics under discussion are based.

Beyond doubt it has been a rather common practice to use statistics technically suitable only with interval (or more restricted) types of scales in analyzing data that can at best be ordinally scaled. Many statisticians consider such usage utterly indefensible and irresponsible. Others, however, feel that such practices can be justified under certain circumstances.[6]

This brief review of some aspects of scaling makes apparent why such strenuous efforts have been made by social scientists to develop methods whereby initially qualitative data can be legitimately transposed into ordinal and interval scales. Early work on ordinal scaling by such persons as Bogardus was largely replaced in the late 1920's and early 1930's by the scaling methods of Thurstone and Likert which seemed to some at the time to offer promise of the holy grail of interval measurement. But growing uneasiness that Thurstone and Likert type scales might not even be ordinal (because there was no certain way of demonstrating that the objects scaled comprised a single dimension or a universe of content, that is, a single well-structured set of attitudes) led to renewed interest in establishing demonstrably ordinal scales. The breakthrough came when Louis Guttman, a mathematical sociologist then with the Research Branch of the United States Army's Information and Education Division, developed the cumulative scaling technique which sometimes bears his name.[7]

In cumulative scaling one seeks to arrange respondents (for example, judges) and stimuli (for example, cases) in a matrix in an effort to determine whether persons who respond affirmatively to a weak stimulus do in fact respond affirmatively to all stronger stimuli — and, in addition, whether persons who respond negatively to a strong stimulus will also respond negatively to all weaker ones. If a single well-structured set of attitudes is shared

---

[6] See Stevens, *On the Theory of Scales of Measurement*, 103 SCIENCE 677 (1946).

[7] See the contributions by Guttman in 4 THE AMERICAN SOLDIER: STUDIES IN SOCIAL PSYCHOLOGY IN WORLD WAR II, chs. 2, 3, 6, 8, 9 (Stouffer ed. 1950) ("Measurement and Prediction").

by all or virtually all respondents, a continuum of stimuli representing varying degrees of intensity should reveal an identifiable point at which each respondent ceases to react affirmatively and begins to react negatively. Table I illustrates such a matrix for six classes of respondents and five stimuli. Each class of respondents constitutes a perfect scale type. As the matrix makes clear, scale type A respondents react affirmatively to all stimuli to which type B respondents react affirmatively and to weaker stimuli as well. Type B respondents hold a similar relationship to type C respondents and so on. These relationships are clearly transitive and asymmetrical, and so the structure of the scale is unquestionably cumulative, or ordinal.

TABLE I

MODEL OF A PERFECT CUMULATIVE SCALE

Classes of Respondents (or Scale types)	INTENSITY OF STIMULI				
	Very Strong	Strong	Moderate	Weak	Very Weak
A	+	+	+	+	+
B	+	+	+	+	−
C	+	+	+	−	−
D	+	+	−	−	−
E	+	−	−	−	−
F	−	−	−	−	−

Should an unexpected response occur (an affirmative where a negative is expected, as in − + − − −, or a negative where an affirmative is expected, as in + − + + +), the response would be considered an inconsistency or error. Perfect consistency is not to be expected in most areas of human endeavor and especially not in adjudication, where competing interests are almost always involved. As Justice Frankfurter observed in the *Dennis* case: [8] "Adjustment of clash of interests which are at once subtle and fundamental is not likely to reveal entire consistency in a series of instances presenting the clash." And so this thorny question necessarily arises: How much inconsistency can be tolerated without destroying the fundamentally cumulative character of a scale? To this problem we shall subsequently return.

---

[8] Dennis v. United States, 341 U.S. 494, 528 (1951).

II. THE POTENTIAL UTILITY OF SCALOGRAM ANALYSIS

Why bother to scale? The discussion is directed toward the potential, rather than the established, utility of scaling judicial decisions because there is serious doubt whether what now passes for the cumulative scaling of judicial decisions is, in any strict sense, cumulative scaling at all. The basis for this doubt will be discussed in the final section of this paper.

As already indicated, cumulative scaling is, first of all, a means for determining whether the votes cast by the members of a court in a group of cases can be arranged in the kind of matrix illustrated in Table I. Let us hypothesize that the members of the United States Supreme Court share a set of attitudes toward civil liberties which can be characterized in this way. That is to say, all Justices will vote to upset strong deprivations of civil liberties, some will vote to upset moderate deprivations as well, and one or two Justices will vote to upset not only strong and moderate deprivations of civil liberties but also weak ones. To test this hypothesis it is necessary to arrange the cases containing civil liberties issues on a continuum in such a manner that varying degrees of intensity are represented in ordinal fashion. The strongest deprivations will fall at one end of the continuum and the weakest deprivations at the other. Then one must be able to classify the judges who participated in these cases in accordance with perfect, or nearly perfect, scale types. If one cannot set up a matrix of this character, such as the matrix illustrated in the model, then one does not have a cumulative scale, and the behavior of the judges cannot be accounted for in terms of the single hypothesized dimension.

If, on the other hand, a cumulative scale does result, then impressive evidence in support of the hypothesis has been obtained. To be sure, such evidence gives no absolute assurance that the hypothesis is true. There may be alternative explanations for the scale. Should claims by Communist defendants in Smith Act and deportation cases result in a cumulative scale, it would not necessarily follow that the judges decided the cases as they did because Communists as such were involved. Among the alternative possibilities might be that the Communists were treated as criminal defendants, or as individuals asserting free speech deprivations, or as persons claiming that their civil liberties had been violated. Like the blood test for paternity, cumulative scaling can eliminate erroneous hypotheses, but it cannot by itself demonstrate the existence of true ones.

Yet, in another sense, the blood test for paternity is not an entirely apt analogy, for the blood test is not used to demonstrate the existence of the child in question. However, when a set of cases can be made to scale, this very phenomenon constitutes strong evidence that a single well-structured set of attitudes (whatever its proper label) is shared by the members of a court.

Now let us assume that the votes cast by the members of an appellate court in a given set of cases have in fact been arranged so as to constitute a nearly perfect cumulative scale. What then? For one thing, the probable behavior of the justices in cases not yet before the court can be predicted. All that is necessary if one is to do this is to be able to indicate where a pending case falls on the intensity continuum. To return to the model in Table I once again, if a case can be said to fall in the strong intensity category, then judges who belong to scale types A, B, C, and D should respond affirmatively and those in scale types E and F negatively. Or, if a case belongs in the very weak intensity category, only type A should render affirmative responses.

In addition, some consequences of changes in a court's membership should be predictable. Let us suppose that an appellate court of nine members can be scaled in civil liberties cases in such a manner that two judges each belong to scale types A, B, and F and one each to scale types C, D, and E. Deprivations of moderate intensity would then be decided 5–4 in favor of civil liberties claims and those of weak intensity 5–4 against such claims. Under those circumstances if a type A, B, or C judge left the court and was replaced by a type D, E, or F judge, moderate deprivations of civil liberties would prove acceptable to a majority. But if a type D, E, or F judge was replaced by an A or B type, even weak deprivations would be reversed on appeal.

Beyond all this, there is another way in which the cumulative scaling of an appellate court's decisions could prove valuable. If a scale could be constructed for each of several sets of judicial attitudes, then statistics appropriate for ordinal measurement might be used. What is more, there are even circumstances under which the much more powerful statistics assuming interval measurement might be justified.

III. An Evaluation

As suggested above, I am not persuaded that efforts to scale appellate court decisions ordinally have actually resulted in acceptable cumulative scales. In this section I shall set forth the reasons for my skepticism.

The scale type to which a judge is assigned is rather obviously a function of the way in which cases are positioned on the stimulus continuum. That is to say, if the ordering of the cases on the stimulus continuum were substantially rearranged, the scale types to which some judges were assigned would also be apt to change. It is equally obvious that one cannot seriously claim to have ranked the respondents (judges) ordinally if the cases are not also ordinally positioned on the intensity continuum. Hence the method for insuring that the cases have in fact been ordinally ranked is a matter of critical importance and requires close scrutiny.

Procedures in ordering cases seem to be of two general types. One type has been spelled out in great detail by Schubert.[9] The most important of the numerous rules he presents are these:

1. Cases decided by a full court are ordered in accordance with the division by which the court decided them, that is, 9–0, 8–1, 7–2, and so forth.

2. Cases decided by less than a full court are grouped with the most nearly corresponding divisions of the full court, for example, 8–0 with 9–0 and 8–1.

3. No case decided by a majority of positive votes may be classified with a group decided by a majority of negative votes. That is, a 3–4 decision may be grouped with 4–5 or 3–6 decisions, but not with 5–4 or 6–3 decisions.

The formulation of Schubert's rules was apparently dictated by a concern for replacing the generous range of intuition and aesthetic tastes in scale construction with techniques leading to an invariant matrix for any set of cases. And his rules are successful in doing this most of the time. These rules do not, however, necessarily aid in ranking the cases in accordance with the intensity of the hypothesized stimulus each presumably provides. Nor do I understand Schubert to claim that his rules do this. The first two rules can only assure that any given case is ordinally positioned on the intensity continuum if one is prepared to as-

---

[9] SCHUBERT, QUANTITATIVE ANALYSIS OF JUDICIAL BEHAVIOR 280–86 (1959).

sume that the magnitude of the division within an appellate court is of the following character: sharp splits (5–4, 4–5, 6–3, 3–6) involve issues of moderate intensity, whereas unanimous or nearly unanimous decisions involve issues of either very strong (9–0, 8–0, 8–1, 7–1) or very weak (0–9, 0–8, 1–8, 1–7) intensity. But surely such divisions can often be explained just as plausibly in a variety of other ways. To take but one illustration, whether a civil liberties issue of high, moderate, or low intensity results in a unanimously favorable, unanimously unfavorable, or sharply divided court can well depend on the presence of other dimensions such as serious jurisdictional problems, federalism, the overruling of recent precedent, the exercise of executive power in crisis, a competing civil liberty, and the like. *Screws, Classic, Korematsu, Bartkus, Francis v. Resweber, Dennis, Yates, Zorach v. Clauson, Betts v. Brady, Gideon, Mapp, Gobitis, Braunfeld,* and *Engel v. Vitale* provide examples of the kinds of situations that I have in mind.[10]

It is not surprising then that the application of Schubert's rules can lead to odd results. Spaeth utilized these rules in constructing his W matrix. The W matrix contains the votes cast by Supreme Court Justices in fifty-one nonunanimous cases involving labor unions decided in the 1953–1959 Terms.[11] The matrix ranks the Justices in accordance with the favorability of their attitudes toward unionism as follows: Douglas, Black, Warren, Brennan, Clark, Burton, Reed, Stewart, Jackson, Minton, Frankfurter, Harlan, and Whittaker. One should, therefore, be entitled to conclude that Clark supported unions whenever Burton did (and Stewart whenever Frankfurter did) and on some additional occasions as well. But in fact this does not occur. Harlan favored the unions in five cases when Frankfurter voted against them and opposed

---

[10] See, in this connection, the discussion of *Bartkus v. Illinois* in GROSSMAN, LAWYERS AND JUDGES 14–17 (1965). The citations for the cases referred to are as follows: Gideon v. Wainwright, 372 U.S. 335 (1963); Engel v. Vitale, 370 U.S. 421 (1962); Mapp v. Ohio, 367 U.S. 643 (1961); Braunfeld v. Brown, 366 U.S. 599 (1961); Bartkus v. Illinois, 359 U.S. 121 (1959); Yates v. United States, 354 U.S. 298 (1957); Zorach v. Clauson, 343 U.S. 306 (1952); Dennis v. United States, 341 U.S. 494 (1951); Louisiana *ex rel.* Francis v. Resweber, 329 U.S. 459 (1947); Screws v. United States, 325 U.S. 91 (1945); Korematsu v. United States, 323 U.S. 214 (1944); Betts v. Brady, 316 U.S. 455 (1942); United States v. Classic, 313 U.S. 299 (1941); and Minersville School District v. Gobitis, 310 U.S. 586 (1940).

[11] Spaeth, *Warren Court Attitudes Toward Business: The "B" Scale,* in JUDICIAL DECISION-MAKING 79, 84–85 (Schubert ed. 1963).

them only twice when Frankfurter supported them. Similarly, Stewart voted for unions on one occasion when Harlan went against them, but in three other cases just the reverse was true. This same phenomenon occurs in regard to some other Justices on the W matrix.

Moreover, Schubert's rules are not followed by Schmidhauser, Ulmer, or for that matter by Schubert himself.[12] Apparently the reason is that the rules do not always lead to a matrix which minimizes the number of inconsistent votes. What these scholars appear to do is to shuffle cases and Justices about until they minimize the total number of inconsistencies and consequently maximize certain measures conventionally used for determining the existence of a cumulative scale. The shuffling technique of matrix construction creates problems no less severe than do Schubert's rules. One is that several quite different arrangements of cases and Justices can frequently be made to yield the same number of minimum inconsistencies. As I have demonstrated elsewhere,[13] one may not be able to reduce the number of inconsistencies in Spaeth's W scale, but one can change the order of most of the cases and the rank order of ten of the thirteen judges without increasing the number of inconsistencies at all. The seriousness of this defect (widely different matrices with the same minimum number of inconsistencies) is all too evident when one recalls that a major purpose of cumulative scaling is to set reliably the rank order of the judges in regard to a single attitudinal dimension.

Apart from questions related to the rank ordering of the judges, there is another difficulty which is logically prior and intrinsically more important: Does even a unique matrix constructed by the shuffling technique provide sufficient basis for concluding that the members of a court share a single well-structured set of attitudes? Those committed to cumulative scaling proceed on the assumption that any matrix which satisfies certain conventional criteria *ipso facto* fulfills the requirements of cumulative scaling. Let us consider these criteria.

The two conventional methods used by students of judicial

---

[12] See the works by Schmidhauser and Ulmer, *supra* note 1. See also, *e.g.*, the matrices in SCHUBERT, THE JUDICIAL MIND 104–07, 109 (1965).

[13] Tanenhaus, "Scaling," in MURPHY & TANENHAUS, WORKING PAPERS FOR THE INTER-UNIVERSITY CONSORTIUM FOR POLITICAL RESEARCH SEMINAR IN JUDICIAL BEHAVIOR D 14–15, TABLES II and III (July 1963, mimeo.).

behavior for determining whether a set of cases has been ordered in accord with a single dimension are known as the Coefficient of Reproducibility (CR), and the Coefficient of Scalability (S). CR is the percentage of all votes cast which are consistent. S is the percentage of potentially inconsistent votes that are in fact consistent. CR's of 90 per cent and S's of 60 to 65 per cent are conventionally regarded as sufficient to establish the existence of ordinal scales. Now it is certainly true that CR's and S's much below these arbitrary, if conventional, levels do demonstrate that one or more Justices cannot be ordered in terms of a single dimension. But is the reverse a sound inference? I think not.

For one thing, as is now widely recognized, CR tends to be high if very many unanimous or nearly unanimous cases are included (8–1, 7–1, 7–2, 6–2, 2–6, etc.). In fact, S was designed to offset situations of this kind. But S itself tends to be high if very many sharply divided cases (6–3, 5–4, 4–5, 3–6) were decided by identical groups of judges. One could, for example, take the dozen or so civil liberties cases decided 5–4 by identical groups of Supreme Court Justices (Frankfurter, Clark, Burton, Harlan, and Whittaker versus Douglas, Black, Warren, and Brennan) in Volumes 353–357 of the United States Reports, add to them the fifteen other cases decided in May 1958 and have an S in excess of 85 per cent. Nor is this a unique phenomenon.

It is rather easy to contrive nonsensical matrices with conventionally acceptable S coefficients. A combined matrix of Schubert's aliens' claims cases [14] and Spaeth's W cases for the 1953–1955 Terms yields an S of .87, cases during the 1957 Term authored by Burton and Clark an S of .70, cases during the same Term coming from the Second, Third, and Fourth Circuits an S of .66, and cases decided in May 1957 and May 1958 an S of .66. Perhaps a final and more esoteric illustration will serve to make the point. If one takes all the cases in Volume 355 of the United States Reports handed down on days of the month divisible by three, and then classifies them so that a favorable vote is assigned when a Justice supported petitioners (or appellants) with even docket numbers or opposed those with odd docket numbers, and a negative vote for the reverse behavior, one obtains an S of .62. Conventional levels of the already largely discredited CR, or the more highly regarded S, however useful they may be in other

---

[14] SCHUBERT, *op. cit. supra* note 9, at 299.

fields,[15] cannot in themselves establish the existence of a unidimensional continuum. Something more is needed.

This critique, if at all sound, raises serious doubts that the so-called scaling of appellate court behavior is actually cumulative scaling at all. But I do not wish to conclude on so negative a note. I certainly do not wish to imply that all, or even most, of the inferences Schmidhauser, Schubert, Spaeth, and Ulmer have drawn from the matrices they have constructed are unsound. Their inferences are questionable only insofar as they actually require that the cases and hence the judges have been ranked in strictly ordinal fashion. On the contrary, the commentary by these scholars is always imaginative and often penetrating. Schubert's monumental study, *The Judicial Mind*, is certainly a case in point. It seems to me that anyone who takes the trouble to study their published work, including that which relies heavily on what they consider to be cumulative scaling, cannot but enhance his understanding of appellate court behavior.

---

[15] For a discussion of research involving the scaling of legislative roll-call votes see JEWELL & PATTERSON, THE LEGISLATIVE PROCESS IN THE UNITED STATES ch. 21 (1966).

QUANTITATIVE ANALYSIS OF FACT-PATTERNS IN CASES AND THEIR IMPACT ON JUDICIAL DECISIONS

Fred Kort *

Studying the dependence of court decisions on facts can be clearly associated with traditional conceptions of the judicial process. There are, however, salient problems in the relationship between facts and decisions which cannot be solved by conventional methods. Such problems must be attacked by mathematical and statistical methods which have been extensively employed in the behavioral sciences. These methods are not limited to research on social backgrounds of judges, their values, and their individual positions as members of appellate courts. It has recently been suggested that the process of decision-making on the basis of relevant facts involves an attitude of the judge toward his responsibility which may be examined in the same manner as other judicial attitudes.[1] If this view is accepted, the study of the dependence of decisions on facts could rely on methods that are also appropriate for the study of other aspects of judicial behavior. But even if traditional conceptions of the relationship of court decisions to facts are preferred, mathematical and statistical methods provide insights which otherwise cannot be obtained.

The use of mathematical and statistical methods yields such insights in areas of law where comprehensive sets of facts have been specified by appellate courts as relevant and controlling for reaching decisions. In such areas of law, it has been stated by courts that some combinations of the facts would lead to decisions in favor of one party to the dispute and that other combinations would result in decisions for the opposing party. Beyond the association of *some* combinations of facts with decisions which already have been reached, it is not known, however, what decisions can be expected on the basis of *other* combinations of the specified

---

* Professor of Political Science, University of Connecticut. Research Associate, Computation Center, Massachusetts Institute of Technology. Ph.B., Northwestern, 1947, M.A., 1950, Ph.D., 1950.

[1] SCHUBERT, THE JUDICIAL MIND — THE ATTITUDES AND IDEOLOGIES OF SUPREME COURT JUSTICES 1946–1963 (1965).

facts. For example, in the involuntary confession cases under the due process clause of the fourteenth amendment, the Supreme Court has clearly stated that each decision depends on the particular circumstances surrounding the interrogation of each petitioner. Workmen's compensation cases provide another example: reviewing courts have indicated that an award or denial of compensation must be decided on the basis of such facts as the nature of the injury, the circumstances under which the accident occurred and became known, and the health record of the claimant prior to the injury. In both of these areas of adjudication recurring relationships between certain fact configurations and decisional patterns can be identified. A more difficult question is to predict the decisions that other combinations of these facts would justify.

In recent years several studies have attempted to predict decisions by using mathematical and statistical techniques.[2] But a serious problem confronts the scholar in this area: he must identify which facts appellate courts accept as controlling from lower court records and appellate briefs. The problem thus presents two aspects: (1) the acceptance or rejection of facts by appellate courts from lower court records and appellate briefs, and (2) the dependence of the decisions of appellate courts on facts that have been accepted as controlling.

---

[2] This author attempted to analyze the right to counsel cases under the "special circumstances" rule of Betts v. Brady, 316 U.S. 455 (1942). See Kort, *Predicting Supreme Court Decisions Mathematically: A Quantitative Analysis of the "Right to Counsel" Cases*, 51 AM. POL. SCI. REV. 1 (1957). Later studies, relying on factor analysis and a system of simultaneous equations, have dealt with the Supreme Court's treatment of right to counsel and involuntary confession cases and with the Connecticut Supreme Court's workmen's compensation decisions. See Kort, *The Quantitative Content Analysis of Judicial Opinions*, PROD (now Am. Behavioral Scientist), March 1960, p. 11; Kort, *Content Analysis of Judicial Opinions and Rules of Law*, in JUDICIAL DECISION-MAKING 133 (Schubert ed. 1963). Simple correlation methods have been suggested as another solution of the problem. See Nagel, *Using Simple Calculations To Predict Judicial Decisions*, Am. Behavioral Scientist, Dec. 1960, p. 24. One scholar has devised a predictive system based on Boolean algebra. See Lawlor, *Foundations of Logical Legal Decision Making*, Modern Uses of Logic in Law, June 1963, p. 98. For a comparison of this method with the method of simultaneous equations, see Kort, *Simultaneous Equations and Boolean Algebra in the Analysis of Judicial Decisions*, 28 LAW & CONTEMP. PROB. 143 (1963). Discriminant analysis has also been applied to the search and seizure cases; see Ulmer, *Quantitative Analysis of Judicial Processes: Some Practical and Theoretical Applications*, 28 LAW & CONTEMP. PROB. 164, 165–76 (1963).

I. The Acceptance or Rejection of Facts
That Control Judicial Decisions From Lower
Court Records and Appellate Briefs

Many legal realists argue that the acceptance or rejection of facts by appellate courts cannot be reduced to regular patterns.[3] If the contrary can be shown, however, the prediction of the acceptance or rejection of facts, and ultimately the prediction of decisions, will become possible. As an initial hypothesis, it can be stated that the acceptance of a fact by an appellate court depends upon identifiable conditions surrounding the presentation of the fact in the briefs and record below. These conditions can be stated as follows: the appellate court will accept the fact *if and only if* it appears at one or more of the stages which the lower court records and appellate briefs represent, *or* is not denied at one or more of these stages, *or* one or a combination of other facts also is accepted by the appellate court. A specific application of this compound statement may be exemplified by the involuntary confession cases decided by the Supreme Court. The alleged fact that the defendant had not been advised of his right to remain silent is accepted by the Supreme Court *if and only if* (a) the fact appears in a dissenting opinion of the lower appellate court *and* in the respondent's brief to the Supreme Court *and* is not denied in the allegations of the respondent in the transcript of the record *and* in the opinion of the lower court, *or* (b) it appears in the allegations of the respondent in the transcript of the record *and* in a dissenting opinion of the lower court *and* in the brief of the petitioner to the Supreme Court *and* is not denied in the respondent's brief, *or* (c) it appears in the petitioner's brief to the Supreme Court *and* is not denied in the opinion of the lower court *and* in a dissenting opinion, *and* the alleged fact that the petitioner was not advised of his right to counsel also is accepted by the Supreme Court.

The complexity of this statement directs attention to the need for a more concise formulation. Such a formulation can be obtained by using the algebraic notation devised by the nineteenth century British mathematician George Boole — Boolean algebra — first applied to the analysis of judicial decisions by Reed C. Lawlor.[4] The notation also can be regarded as a form of symbolic

---

[3] See, *e.g.*, Frank, Courts on Trial (1949).

[4] See Lawlor, *supra* note 2; Kort, *Models for the Analysis of Fact-Acceptance by Appellate Courts*, Am. Behavioral Scientist, April 1966, p. 8.

logic. The purpose of the concise formulation is not merely the convenience of relative brevity, but the important objective of reducing the compound statement to a form which permits further analysis.

The compound statement which specifies the conditions under which a fact is accepted by an appellate court — the acceptance rule — can vary considerably for different facts. Initially it is not known which combination of appearances, nonappearances, or denials of a fact, as well as the acceptance of other facts, provides the acceptance rule for the fact. For example, in both the involuntary confession cases and the Connecticut workmen's compensation cases over one billion such combinations are possible for each relevant fact. Although not every possible combination needs to be examined to determine which compound statement can be correctly inferred for each fact from the applicable case,[5] the number of combinations which must be examined makes human inspection prohibitive. However, the systematic search for the applicable compound statement can be performed by a digital computer — in fact, it was in this way that results for the Connecticut workmen's compensation cases and for the involuntary confession cases were obtained.

Although the compound statements identify the possible conditions for the acceptance or rejection of relevant facts by appellate courts, and thus provide a basis for prediction, two limitations must be noted. One is that the statements cannot feasibly take into account multiple manifestations of the appearance or denial of a fact, such as several accidents in a workmen's compensation case, some or all of which could be denied at various stages. Another limitation is that a direct statistical significance test for the compound statements is not available. The need for such a test becomes crucial when prediction of acceptance or rejection is attempted. For these reasons, another method has to be considered.

This other method employs a system of equations. Each case is represented by an equation, in which an index denoting the acceptance or rejection of a fact by an appellate court is set equal to the combination of appearances, nonappearances, and denials

---

[5] For an explanation of why not every possible combination would have to be examined, see Kort, *Simultaneous Equations and Boolean Algebra in the Analysis of Judicial Decisions*, 28 LAW & CONTEMP. PROB. 143, 153–56 (1963).

of the fact at the preceding stages.[6] The weights of the fact at the various stages — in the sense of how persuasive its appearance at the respective stages is toward its acceptance by the appellate court — are the *unknowns* in the equations. As the equations are solved, the weights are determined. To be sure, the complex procedures which are required for the solution of the equations again necessitate the use of a computer, especially because there is a separate system of equations for each fact. By using the weights in a case not previously encountered, one can predict for each fact an acceptance or rejection that would be consistent with the established pattern of past cases. Although it may not be possible to predict every acceptance or rejection correctly, a statistical test for determining whether or not the predicted results are significant is available. For example, in the involuntary confession cases and the Connecticut workmen's compensation cases the test has shown that the results that were obtained are highly significant.

II. The Dependence of Appellate Court Decisions on Facts That Have Been Accepted as Controlling

The methods which can be used for analyzing the acceptance or rejection of facts by appellate courts also can be employed in examining the dependence of the decisions of these courts on the facts that they have accepted as controlling. The initial approach is essentially the same. Starting from the hypothesis that a decision in favor of the aggrieved party requires the occurrence of specified conditions regarding the facts accepted by the appellate court, the following compound statement can be formulated. The decision is in favor of the aggrieved party *if and only if* facts in one of several specified combinations have been accepted by the appellate court.[7] In its specific applications this compound statement can assume forms amounting to several billions. But, through the use of a computer, it becomes possible to provide a basis for predicting decisions by deriving the correct compound statement from past cases.

---

[6] For a mathematical exposition of these equations, see Kort, *supra* note 4, at 9.

[7] For an exposition of this general compound statement in Boolean algebra and its applications, see Kort, *supra* note 5, at 150–52.

The alternative method of a system of equations also has to be considered here. Again, each case is represented by an equation. In this instance, an index which denotes the decision (in favor or against the party seeking redress) is set equal to the combination of facts that have been accepted by the appellate court.[8] The weights of the accepted facts — in the sense of how persuasive they are toward a decision in favor of the aggrieved party — are the *unknowns* in the equations. It may be impossible, for want of sufficient available data, to solve these equations.[9] This problem can be attacked, however, by restating the facts in terms of *factors*, and by employing *factor analysis*.[10] In the involuntary confession cases, for example, some of the facts which have been accepted as controlling by the Supreme Court include a delay in the formal presentation of charges, the incommunicado detention of the defendant, and the failure to advise the defendant of his right to remain silent or his right to counsel. These facts can be restated in terms of a factor described as "a tactic to keep the defendant in isolation and uninformed about the preceeding against him." This would be an example of the intuitive meaning of restating facts in terms of factors. It should be noted, however, that applicable factors actually are found by relying *exclusively* on the mathematical technique which factor analysis employs. It also should be noted that — in addition to solving the problem encountered in the original equations — factor analysis fully explores the mutual dependence or independence of the facts. For this reason, it always is advisable to attempt to restate the facts in terms of factors. For the same reason, it also would be irrelevant to say that factor analysis does not increase the predictability of the decisions.

On the basis of the restatement of the accepted facts in terms of factors, the original equations now can be restated as new equations, with indices denoting the decisions set equal to the

---

[8] For a mathematical exposition of these equations, see *id.* at 144–48.

[9] In many situations, the equations which represent the cases do not contain sufficient information for a unique solution, as a result of the particular combinations of facts in the available cases.

[10] There are various methods of factor analysis. Hotelling's method of factoring, also known as the principal components or principal axes method, is the most desirable method for locating the factors in terms of which the facts can be restated. See THURSTONE, MULTIPLE-FACTOR ANALYSIS 480–503 (1947). For restating the combination of facts in terms of factors in each case, see HARMAN, MODERN FACTOR ANALYSIS 338–56 (1960).

various combinations of factors in the cases.[11] The weights of the factors — again in the sense of how persuasive they are toward a decision in favor or against the aggrieved party — are the *unknowns* in the equations. The weights of the factors are found by solving the equations. As new cases arise, the applicable facts can be reduced to the factors which have been identified, and the decisions can be predicted.

Of primary interest to the present discussion is the combination of the methods for analyzing the acceptance of facts and the methods for exploring the dependence of decisions on facts. Such a combination of methods makes it possible to predict first the acceptance or rejection of facts by appellate courts from lower court records and appellate briefs, and then the decisions of the appellate courts on the basis of the accepted facts. A comprehensive computer program which implements this combination of methods has been completed.[12] It has been applied initially to the involuntary confession and Connecticut workmen's compensation cases, with highly significant results. The computer program and the methods it implements are, however, general and may be applied to any area of law in which fact-patterns determine judicial decisions.

III. Purposes, Limitations, and Implications of the Proposed Methods

The purposes of the proposed methods must be understood not only in terms of their effective combination for prediction, but also in terms of their potentials for analyzing separately the two aspects of the problem under discussion. With regard to the acceptance and rejection of facts by appellate courts, the methods offer insights into matters about which there has been considerable speculation. Since the emergence of "fact-skepticism" in the framework of legal realism, there has been a widespread belief that courts pay relatively little attention to facts. The application

---

[11] For a mathematical exposition of these equations, see Kort, *supra* note 5, at 149–50.

[12] The program has been developed by this author with extensive use of the IBM 7040 at the Computer Center of the University of Connecticut and with partial use of the IBM 7094 at the Computation Center of the Massachusetts Institute of Technology. The support of this research by the Social Science Research Council and the opportunity of using the computer facilities are gratefully acknowledged.

of the proposed methods has refuted such a belief in at least some areas of law.

With regard to the dependence of decisions on facts, the proposed methods provide a precise and exhaustive distinction between combinations of facts that lead to decisions in favor of one party to the dispute and combinations of facts that lead tô decisions in favor of the opposing party. Thus, the methods offer information about the content and the application of rules of law which verbal statements of these rules do not provide. The given examples show that courts employ rules which state that the decisions shall be made on the basis of combinations of facts. The verbal statements of these rules specify which facts shall be regarded as relevant but do not specify which combinations of these facts call for a decision in favor of the party seeking redress and which do not. This is the information which the proposed methods can provide.

It already has been seen that prediction is another purpose of the proposed methods. Prediction is possible only if it can be assumed that the patterns of consistency in past cases — with regard to the acceptance of facts as well as with regard to the decisions — will continue in the future. The proposed methods are not designed to predict doctrinal changes and the adoption of new rules of law. Furthermore, prediction does not apply to a case in which a fact *not previously encountered* appears, although a series of such cases provides a basis for the prediction of subsequent decisions. Thus the methods can demonstrate their validity, provided that their limitations are clearly recognized and understood, and that claims never made on their behalf are not carelessly attributed to them.

It should be noted that, in examining past cases by means of the proposed methods, no assumption is made regarding the existence or nonexistence of consistent patterns in the acceptance of facts or in decisions based on facts. Whether or not consistency does exist in a given area of adjudication is determined by the use of the methods. If consistent patterns cannot be identified, it must be concluded that judicial action in the given area of law cannot be understood in terms of the dependence of decisions on facts. If, on the other hand, consistent patterns are found, an important implication of the proposed methods is apparent. Should it be possible to predict only later cases from earlier cases, the underlying pattern of consistency could be explained in terms of stare decisis. But if earlier cases could be predicted from later ones, adherence to precedent would have to be explained in terms of an independent — although convergent — recognition and acceptance of similar standards of justice by different judges at different times. Thus not only the existence of consistent patterns but also the basis for their consistency can be evaluated.

Where patterns of consistency in the acceptance of facts and in corresponding decisions appear to be absent, other explanations of judicial action obviously must be given. Such explanations could be obtained from studies concerned with other aspects of the judicial process, such as the characteristics and changes in the attitudes and values of judges, their social backgrounds, and their individual positions as members of appellate courts. The possibility of effective coordination of these various endeavors remains an open question. Gustav Bergmann called attention to the fact that free-falling bodies, the inclined plane, and the pendulum originally were explained in terms of three separate empirical laws.[13] Later, these three phenomena were regarded as special cases of a set of general laws — the laws of mechanics — and a scientific theory replaced the empirical laws. It is not inconceivable that similar developments will eventually lead to a scientific theory of the judicial process.

---

[13] See Bergmann, *An Empiricist's System of the Sciences*, 59 THE SCIENTIFIC MONTHLY 140, 144 (1944)

AN AFTERWORD: SCIENCE AND THE JUDICIAL PROCESS

Lon L. Fuller *

Science must proceed by abstraction. It cannot deal with everything at once. To achieve its objectives it must isolate — experimentally or conceptually — a limited number of interacting phenomena from the larger field in which they commonly operate.

The necessity to work with, and to think in terms of, simplified models is as much a necessity in the social sciences as it is in physics. The difference is, however, that it is hard to define in the social sciences just what is being abstracted and therefore difficult to know what corrections to make when formal theories are applied to real life. There is little danger that the physicist who calculates what would happen in the absence of friction will suppose, when he turns to man-made machinery, that it also operates without friction. In the social sciences the transition from abstract models to the actualities of social living is not so simple. Though it is probably safe to say that in the social sciences the degree of abstraction exceeds by far anything normally encountered in the physical sciences, the very bulk and complexity of this abstraction makes it difficult to state plainly just what has been left out. This has the unfortunate result that as the potential damage done by misapplications of theory increases, the likelihood that such misapplications will occur also increases. Sometimes, accordingly, the only safe course is to disregard theories derived from abstract models when one is confronted with the problems of actual human existence.

It certainly cannot be said that the contributors to this symposium are unaware of the pitfalls just suggested. On the contrary, each of them is at pains to warn his readers that in one way or another he has dealt with the judicial process in terms that are artificially simplified. However, I am not sure that all of the contributors have made clear the full measure of the abstractions on which their conclusions rest. And even if the scattered concessions made by the five contributors were, in com-

---

* Carter Professor of General Jurisprudence, Harvard University. AB., Stanford, 1924, J.D., 1926.

bination, sufficient to cover the field, there would still be some utility in putting them into a more systematic form. At any rate this is what I shall attempt in the first part of my commentary.

I

At the outset it will be well to set off the articles of Murphy and Krislov against those of Grossman, Kort, and Tanenhaus. The first two writers are essentially concerned with analyzing processes of collegial decision. They seek a better understanding of what goes on when judges confer, exchange views, and finally make some disposition of the case, whether it be by a unanimous decision or by the majority vote of a divided court. Murphy and Krislov are concerned with the prediction of the decision of future cases only as a by-product of understanding.

Grossman, Kort, and Tanenhaus, on the other hand, are directly concerned with attaining what has been called "predictive knowledge." They begin by making certain assumptions about the influences that may shape judicial decisions and about the particular ways in which those influences may operate. These assumptions are then tested by asking whether, had they been used to predict later decisions, the predictions thus made would have been accurate in a significant number of the decisions actually reached. The term "postdiction" has been suggested as an apt designation for this testing of assumptions by a retrospective use of them to "predict" decisions already reached.[1] Naturally it is hoped that if the assumptions prove themselves effective in this imaginary employment they will be equally useful in predicting decisions that actually lie in the future.

In turning now to a more detailed analysis of the individual papers, let me begin with that of Professor Murphy. For insight into the ways in which collective judicial decisions are reached Murphy turns to the results of what is called small-group research. This branch of sociology (or, if you will, of social psychology) probably involves the most extensive application of the experimental method ever made in the social sciences. The technique is essentially simple. Small experimental groups (usually of students) are brought together and given problems to solve

---

[1] See Nagel, *Predicting Court Cases Quantitatively*, 63 Mich. L. Rev. 1411, 1422 (1965).

or are asked to reach certain kinds of decisions. A record is kept, step by step, of the group's progress toward its goal. Various elements in the situation may be manipulated by the experimenter. For example, in one case, communication within the group may be artificially limited or may be subjected to formal rules. In another case, the group may be left to devise its own forms of internal communication, the object being to see how the participants will themselves shape these forms to the demands of the task assigned.

The method is scientifically unpretentious and is generally innocent of mathematical complexities. Murphy not only makes clear what insights useful for an understanding of judicial decisions may be derived from small-group research but also is at pains to show the limitations of this source of help. The abstractions and simplifications demanded by the method are, in any event, sufficiently obvious not to require detailed analysis here.

Like Murphy, Krislov is primarily interested in understanding collegial processes of decision. Instead of drawing on small-group research, however, he turns chiefly to what is called game theory. This subject can perhaps best be described as a branch of mathematical economics. Its most fruitful (or at least its most uncomplicated) application is to what are called zero-sum games, "games" being understood in this context as running all the way from matching pennies to shooting to kill at high noon. Zero-sum games are games in which the opposition of interests is complete, so that one man's gain must be the other man's loss. (The sum involved is an algebraic sum, so that plus four combined with minus four produces a sum of zero.) Even in zero-sum games the theory does not purport to offer a strategy for total victory, but only principles by which to establish a kind of base line of comparative safety against whatever form of attack may come from the other side. In cooperative games, such as relationships of exchange, where it is possible for both parties to gain, the teachings of game theory are less clear. Theoretically it can be directed toward maximizing gains on both sides. The social implications of this possibility so moved one British philosopher that he ends his book with the hopeful conjecture: [2] "Perhaps in

---

[2] BRAITHWAITE, THEORY OF GAMES AS A TOOL FOR THE MORAL PHILOSOPHER 55 (1963). It might be observed that the methods of what is called welfare economics are also directed toward a maximization of private advantage. See

another three hundred years' time economic and political and other branches of moral philosophy will bask in radiation from a source — theory of games of strategy — whose prototype was kindled round the poker tables of Princeton."

At the more modest level on which Krislov pitches his suggestions, what contribution can game theory make to an understanding of collegial judicial decisions? Plainly no matter how acute hostilities within a court may become, it is unlikely that judges will often be reduced to playing zero-sum games with one another. Can that part of game theory which deals with cooperative games help us to understand the judicial process? Offhand one might be inclined to suppose that the strategy of judges toward one another is too transparent an activity to profit from sophisticated mathematical analysis. But it is a fact that we often play more subtle and complex games with one another than we realize. Mutually advantageous relations of reciprocity are often not fully perceived by the parties who enter into them and profit from them. If game theory can bring to consciousness the intuitive calculations from which such relationships arise, it may enrich our understanding of judicial ploys and counterploys.

The chief danger in any application of game theory to judicial decision-making lies in the fact that it is essentially a theory of satisfactions that are, broadly speaking, "economic" in nature, that is, are atomistic and individual. It is concerned with the "pay-off" and not with the rewards of the game itself. As Krislov points out, men play poker not simply to win money, but also for the pleasure of gambling. So judges may derive rewards from collaborative efforts that transcend individual "pay-offs."

There is, however, a more fundamental danger in attempting to analyze judicial behavior in terms of an economic calculus. To see what this danger is we need only recall that what a judge may want (some of us are naïve enough to hope that this is what he will always want) is a decision that is just, proper, and workable. When this driving motor of the judicial process is left out of account, the simplifying distortions of game theory become dangerous in ways not explicitly recognized by Krislov. For surely we cannot give a true account of collaborative judging if we assume that it consists entirely of one-upmanship toward one's colleagues, tempered by a sense of togetherness.

Musgrave, *The Public Interest: Efficiency in the Creation and Maintenance of Material Welfare*, 5 Nomos 107 (1962).

II

The studies reported by Grossman are not concerned with providing any new insight into the process of collegial decision. Instead, they abstract from that process and concentrate on the judicial votes that emerge from it. Their chief concern seems to be to determine to what extent judicial votes reflect dispositions or "values" brought to the bench from the world outside. They ask such questions as whether Republican judges are more likely to vote to nullify the actions of administrative agencies than are their Democratic counterparts. Questions such as these are then subjected to an elaborate testing that may involve Guttman scaling, Boolean algebra, and other mathematical and statistical techniques.

In constructing a program for research of this kind the social scientist confronts the necessity for making three major determinations: (1) He must select the factors to be tested for possible influence on judicial decisions. (2) He must decide how to interpret particular decisions — for example, shall a vote to strike down some administrative regulation of business activity be interpreted as expressing a tendency toward "economic conservatism"? (3) He must choose some appropriate mathematical method for bringing the hypothecated predispositions into relation with the actual judicial behavior of the subject under study.

It should not be supposed that these three determinations are independent of one another or that they would be reached chronologically in the order in which I have stated them. In the total design of the project they will inevitably interact. In determining what extracurial influences to select for study, for example, the researcher will have to ask himself whether a given influence can be converted into terms that are manageable mathematically. On the other hand, in selecting among alternative mathematical procedures he will be likely to select the procedure that seems most congruent with the normal workings of human motivation.

Let us examine in turn each of the major decisions that are involved in research design. The first relates to the choice of the extracurial influences to be studied for their possible influence on judicial decisions. Here one is struck by the conservatism of the researchers. They do not ask whether the judge is for or against vivisection, cremation, nominalism, or organic farming. They do not inquire whether his preferred drink is rye with ginger ale or a vodka martini with a discreet slice of lemon peel. Instead they ask such unimaginative questions as whether he is a Republican or a Democrat, whether he grew up in the city or in the country, and the like.

Things have not always been so, at least in academic legend. In the 'thirties there was much talk of a projected study of the influences affecting decisions at the trial level. The usual trite variables were, of course, to be included — the judge's family background, the nature of his practice before his appointment to the bench, and other like matters. But the program also called for a determination of the manner in which the American flag was displayed in the courtroom and whether the electric wiring of the courthouse carried alternating or direct current. One may rejoice that the days of such blatant pretension to scientific open-mindedness are over. But certainly a finding that direct current is clearly associated with a much higher percentage of acquittals than is alternating current would be more exciting to the imagination than a solemn finding that Republican judges prove themselves on the bench less favorable to labor unions than do their Democratic colleagues.

I shall have occasion later to return to this problem of picking the "independent variables." For the time being I should like merely to record an impression that the attitudes and predispositions selected for study tend to be: (1) not those that fall into complex patterns but those that are thought to fall along a continuum, preferably running from "left" to "right," and (2) those that are "political" in nature in the sense that they may well have influenced the election or appointment of the judge. If this impression is correct, it has an important bearing on the relative success of these studies in uncovering significant associations between extracurial predispositions and judicial "votes." For our appraisal of these studies cannot be realistic if we fail to take account of the possibility that the apparent "success" they achieve is built into the design of the research itself.

When we reach the stage of determining what shall be treated as an "outcome" of the judicial process, to be matched against the judge's "personal values and attitudes," [3] the necessity for simplification and abstraction becomes drastic indeed. In the first place, as Grossman points out, unanimous decisions must be entirely disregarded. The researchers in this field are interested in judicial

---

[3] See pp. 1551–52 *supra*.

divergences, and these must be overtly expressed before they can be taken into account.[4]

In estimating how much is left out when unanimous decisions are excluded from study, one must recall that the impression of solidarity conveyed by such decisions can be quite specious. One of the most perceptive of our state judges once attempted to describe how unanimous decisions look to those who reach them. With his own court, he said, some of these decisions were rated as 90–10, while others might be rated as 51–49, in the second class it having been touch-and-go as to how they would finally be decided. The 90–10 decisions furnish a firm foundation for future development; the principle implicit in them is likely to be extended broadly by analogy. Cases of the second class will be likely to meet an opposite fate. The 51–49 decisions do not necessarily represent any division of opinion among the court; all the judges may have felt substantially the same way and all may have been equally pulled just past the point of indecision in finally reaching a unanimous conclusion. When we thus look behind the blank outer wall of unanimity, it becomes apparent how much judicial preference schedules may be falsified (say, on a Guttman scaling) when unanimous decisions are left out of account. And it should be remembered that the reciprocal adjustments and compromises that go into a unanimous decision may have a carry-over effect on the judge who, in a later case, debates whether to file a dissenting opinion.

The chief distortion introduced by the exclusion of unanimous decisions results, not from the fact that a veil is drawn over divergences that may lie behind such decisions, but from the undue weight it lends to dissents. By entering a dissent the judge gains for himself the opportunity to engage in a very special form of literary exercise, the dissenting opinion. Cardozo has some eloquent things to say about the differences between majority and dissenting opinions:[5]

---

[4] Murphy suggests that investigators in Switzerland might enjoy an advantage in comparison with their American counterparts because court deliberations in their country are required to take place in public. See Murphy, ms. on file at Harvard Law Review, p. 5.

He might have added that in Mexico the deliberations of the Supreme Court are also open to the public. CALAMANDREI, PROCEDURE AND DEMOCRACY 48–49 (1956). One may doubt, however, whether discussions taking place under the strain of such scrutiny would be a very reliable index to real divergences of opinion and belief.

[54] CARDOZO, LAW AND LITERATURE 34 (1931).

Comparatively speaking at least, the dissenter is irresponsible. The spokesman of the court is cautious, timid, fearful of the vivid word, the heightened phrase. . . . The result is to cramp and paralyze. One fears to say anything when the peril of misunderstanding puts a warning finger to the lips. Not so, however, the dissenter. He has laid aside the role of the hierophant, which he will only be too glad to resume when the chances of war make him again the spokesman of the majority. For the moment, he is the gladiator making the last stand against the lions.

In appraising the significance of a dissenting opinion it should be remembered that judges often, tacitly or openly, use the threat of a dissent to obtain some modification in the majority opinion. In deciding how firmly to hold out, the judge inclined toward dissent would be less than human if he were not influenced by the attractiveness of the role in which a dissent casts him. Let us suppose that his appointment to the bench was heralded by *The National Review* or *The Nation* as bringing a wholesome "conservative" or "liberal" influence to the court. The cases he confronts offer him for a long time no opportunity to demonstrate to those who believe in his judicial philosophy that he has not deserted them. In such situations the opportunity to write a dissenting opinion in an appropriate case becomes especially attractive and he is likely to take full advantage of the occasion. Since he is relieved of any complicity in the decision actually reached, he may in fact be moved to show by words that his "personal values and attitudes" remain what they were when he was just a plain, ordinary citizen. In so doing he will please not only his well-wishers but the researchers as well, for his dissent will help to load the figures in favor of a result that the researcher, if he too is human, cannot but hope will emerge from his labors.

In his report on researches of the kind under discussion, Grossman asserts that "these explorations" will "tend to focus on properties of behavior which are amenable to generalization — for example, on judges' votes rather than on their opinions." [6] But this emphasis will surely be misplaced if, as may very well be the case, the primary motive for casting the dissenting *vote* was to procure the opportunity to write the dissenting *opinion*. And it should be remembered that filing a dissent without opinion can

---

[6] See p. 1552 *supra*.

often be interpreted as staking out a claim to write a dissenting opinion on a later and perhaps more auspicious occasion.

But how is it decided — with or without the aid of an opinion — whether a judicial "vote" is "for" or "against" labor unions, economic liberalism, or judicial restraint? Who does the scoring and by what standards? What "personal values and attitudes" does *he* bring to *his* job? How deep an insight does he have into the problems that are being resolved by the judges' "voting"?

A judge votes to declare invalid or unlawful some exercise of power by a labor union. Does this prove he is "against" labor unions? It is quite possible that he has a deep faith in the labor movement, but is convinced that the greatest threat to it lies in irresponsible actions by unions. It may even be that his friendliness toward labor has enabled him to obtain an understanding of such problems denied to those who stand at a greater distance from the battle.

Surely life is not so black-and-white as the students of judicial voting behavior often seem to make it. Harry Shulman's famous Holmes Lecture [7] is regarded by many as the most enlightened statement ever made of the arbitrator's role in labor disputes. Yet another arbitrator, of a national reputation fully equal to that of Shulman's, stated to me that he regarded the views expressed in that lecture as fundamentally inconsistent with collective bargaining. The general counsel of a great labor union once remarked to me that he sometimes wondered why any labor union would ask for the closed shop and why any employer would ever hesitate to grant it. What he had in mind, of course, was the soporific effect of security. I did not take his remark as being intended with literal seriousness. It illustrates, however, some of the complexities of the problems of labor relations as seen by those most directly engaged in them. It is well known to experienced labor arbitrators that unions often bring grievances to arbitration hoping to lose them. This may happen when improved machinery, with new automatic controls, makes it possible for the worker to tend, effectively and without strain, a larger number of machines than he has in the past. When management proposes an increase in the assignment of machines, the worker, frightened by the unfamiliarity of the new equipment, concludes in all good faith that management is trying to hoodwink him into accepting a "stretch

---

[7] Shulman, *Reason, Contract, and Law in Labor Relations*, 68 HARV. L. REV. 999 (1955).

out." The union loyally argues the case for a lower machine assignment. The award, to the satisfaction of everyone but the worker — and ultimately to his satisfaction too — goes in favor of management. In rendering this award should the arbitrator be scored as voting "antilabor"?

Nor are these complexities and ambiguities confined to the labor side of the table. During World War II many representatives of branch factories — on orders from the head office — argued vehemently before the War Labor Board against the inclusion of any maintenance-of-membership clause in their collective bargaining agreements. Often they were considerably relieved when the decision went against this contention.

Admittedly these Janus-faced issues are less likely to come before courts than to be encountered by arbitrators or administrative agencies. But they are often indirectly involved in judicial decisions and when they are one can only hope that the behavioral scientists will understand the game they are scoring.

One of the favorite inquiries in these researches is to ask whether the judge in his decisions betrays a tendency toward economic "liberalism" or "conservatism." A judge votes to strike down the action of a regulatory agency. Shall this be scored as a vote in favor of economic conservatism? The judge may have been convinced of the need for governmental control while being actuated in his decision by a conviction that this control should take the form of enforcing competition rather than supplanting it. In support of this view he might — though it is certainly unlikely that he would — cite the opinion of "progressive" economists in the Communist countries who argue in favor of "market socialism." It is true that the sloganized thinking of the average citizen is blind to such distinctions. But is the judge — who is forced to study complex problems at close range — to be denied the right to rise to a higher level of analysis? And is it always certain that if he does, the social scientist who undertakes to score him will be able to follow him in this ascent?

I am not suggesting, of course, that the researchers into judicial behavior are unaware of this problem. One recent study reports the adoption of a procedure of scoring designed to ensure accuracy and objectivity, in this case as applied to what is called "content analysis":[8] "A panel of three judges — two graduate

---

[8] See Schubert, *Jackson's Judicial Philosophy: An Exploration in Value Analysis*, 59 AM. POL. SCI. REV. 940, 942 (1965).

students and myself — read and scored independently each opinion for the presence of any of a set of 33 substantive categories . . . . Any instances of disagreement in scoring were discussed among the panel of judges until a consensual judgment was reached."

The important issue lies, however, not in the utility of precautions that can reduce the risk of misinterpretation but in the difficulties inherent in the scoring task itself. Presumably it is in response — at least in part — to these difficulties that Kort suggests his variation on the research design. He proposes that judicial votes be viewed as reactions to varying combinations of facts. If, for example, we discover that whenever in a criminal case the fact combination a, b, e, and f is presented to the court a conviction is set aside, while it is affirmed when fact e is absent and its place is taken by fact d, then we shall be on our way to discerning the essential regularities of judicial behavior. We shall be able to penetrate beneath verbal justifications to the patterns actually implicit in judicial voting. The object of research conducted along these lines would seem to be not so much to measure the influence on his decisions of the judge's personal beliefs and attitudes, but to discover what Ihering called "latent rules," [9] that is, unexpressed rules that actually govern the judicial process.

There are serious difficulties in Kort's proposed method which would unsuit it for application to any but the simplest contexts of decision, such as may possibly be presented by workmen's compensation cases. It presupposes a clear distinction between findings of fact and conclusions of law that cannot be drawn. Kort suggests as one variable that may be present in criminal cases, "the alleged fact that the defendant had not been advised of his right to remain silent." [10] Now, "being advised" must mean "being adequately advised." Whether a man is deemed adequately advised involves a conclusion of law. Kort recognizes that his method is "not designed to predict doctrinal changes and the adoption of new rules of law." [11] But a "new rule of law" may quietly emerge by the simple process of tightening up the definition of what will justify a factual finding, let us say, that the defendant was *sufficiently* warned of his rights.

A distinction is often taken between "evidential" facts, on the

---

[9] IHERING, I GEIST DES RÖMISCHEN RECHTS § 3, at 29 (7th & 8th ed. 1924).

[10] See p. 1597 *supra*.

[11] See p. 1602 *supra*.

one hand, and "dispositive" or "operative" facts, on the other.[12] Thus, in judging whether a will is valid a specified degree of sanity is a dispositive fact. A finding whether this dispositive fact exists may be affected by the circumstance that the testator spoke somewhat incoherently when he signed his will. His incoherent speech is, accordingly, an evidential fact. Now plainly Kort is concerned with dispositive facts, and not with the unforeseeable multitude of evidential facts that might tend to prove or disprove particular dispositive facts. Yet when we view the development of the law through time, the distinction between these two kinds of facts often breaks down. What starts as an evidential fact may gradually become, through an explicit or implicit application of presumptions, a dispositive fact.

Generally, the separate elements of a complex set of facts will stand in a relation of interaction among themselves such as to make any merely enumerative treatment impossible. This is well illustrated in cases involving obscenity. The two facts generally considered relevant in such cases are: (1) Is the primary appeal of the book to a prurient interest? (2) Does it have any redeeming social value? These seem on the surface quite distinct from one another. But suppose that the social value of the work, though perceptible to sensitive thinkers, is too obscure to make any impression on the ordinary reader. What then is the rule? Three recent and much discussed decisions of the Supreme Court [13] introduce a new factual variable: Was the book advertised and promoted in such a way as, in effect, to promise the buyer his money's worth in pruriency? How is this fact related to the others? There is some suggestion in one opinion that lurid advertising sets the purchaser's mind toward the book in such a way that for him, at least, its primary appeal will be prurient. Some newspaper editorials have interpreted the decisions as suggesting that when a publisher advertises his book as being salacious an inference is justified that it is in fact salacious. On this interpretation lurid advertising is an evidentiary fact tending to prove the dispositive fact of pruriency. We do not know what the future treatment of these factual variables will be. But as the significance of this or that fact is shifted back and forth we can

---

[12] See Corbin, *Legal Analysis and Terminology*, 29 YALE L.J. 163, 164 (1919).

[13] A Book Named "John Cleland's Memoirs of a Woman of Pleasure" v. Massachusetts, 86 Sup. Ct. 975 (1966); Mishkin v. New York, 86 Sup. Ct. 958 (1966); Ginzburg v. United States, 86 Sup. Ct. 942 (1966).

be certain that what are in effect new rules of law will be emerging. All of this can be summed up in the observation that the "findings of fact" Kort's method would feed into the computers will inevitably carry with them a heavy, but essentially unmeasurable, contamination of law.

There remains for consideration the third major decision facing the researcher, the choice of a mathematical or statistical method suited to revealing significant relations between the judge's "personal values and attitudes" and his judicial "votes." My treatment of this problem will be brief, chiefly because my capacity to deal with it is quite limited. I shall venture the suggestion that the guidepost by which this choice is determined can only be some intuitive or common-sense view of the nature of human motivation. A mathematical method cannot intelligently be selected merely because it is "sophisticated" or offers "a powerful tool of analysis." It can only be wisely chosen because it fits the thing it tests, and in this case that means the way judges actually think and decide. There is no mathematics by which to choose the right mathematics; the pump must first be primed by human insight.

This point can be illustrated by a reference to Tanenhaus's discussion of Guttman scaling. Guttman scaling presupposes a kind of stimulus and response picture of human motivation, with a diminishing response as the stimulus declines. Tanenhaus's ultimate conclusion is adverse to the utility of this model for studies of judicial behavior. Let me point to a limitation of the model, however, that Tanenhaus does not mention. For the scaling to fall into the neat picture presented in his Table I,[14] it is essential to abstract the whole analysis from the dimension of time. Even on the most elementary physiological level a response may be activated in part by a stimulus prior in time to that which appears to release the response, while fatigue may block a response that might otherwise occur. Something like this may occur in the judicial process. A judge, let us say, is "for" labor unions; the word "labor" is in his vocabulary what some semanticists used to call a "yes-word." Since he has been on the bench he has had occasion to vote three times in a row "in favor of" labor. A fourth case involving labor's interests comes up for decision. Theoretically it presents a stronger stimulus to a "pro-labor" vote than any of the preceding three. Our judge, however, has become

---

[14] See p. 1587 *supra.*

worried lest it be thought that he is lacking in the judicial temperament, and may be moved by this concern toward an "anti-labor" vote. Again, suppose the fourth case presents a weaker stimulus than any of the earlier cases, and would normally fall below the breaking point in the judge's support of the "labor position." However, he has written an opinion in each of the preceding cases and finds himself caught up in a web of doctrine that makes it difficult for him to vote "anti-labor" in the fourth case. How such tensions will be resolved we need not conjecture. Their possible existence suggests, however, that the human being cannot be analogized to an electronic machine with a stable and fixed point of response.

My concern here is not to identify any specific defect in Guttman scaling. It is rather to remind the reader of a more general point — namely that the choice of the mathematical procedure to be followed must rest ultimately on a quite unscientific conception of the qualities of human motivation as it operates in judicial decisions.

So much, then, by way of commentary on the problems that must be solved in designing and carrying out a program of research into judicial "voting." This brings us to the question: How shall we appraise the results of this kind of research? One can say in general: a trite finding tells us nothing we did not already know with reasonable assurance, a bizarre finding is intellectually indigestible, a slightly off-beat finding can profitably set our minds to work trying to figure out how to explain it. As illustrations of these three kinds of findings one may mention in order: the common finding that Democratic judges tend more than Republicans to "favor labor," a hypothetical finding that direct current in the walls of the criminal court room produces acquittals, an actual finding that Democratic judges tend to favor the wife "in divorce settlement cases." [15]

We may say then that in any program of research of the sort we have been discussing there are four crucial turning points. We must determine what "personal values and attitudes" our judge has and which of these are likely to influence his judicial voting. We must find some way to determine what his votes as a judge mean in terms of the values and attitudes they express. We must adopt some mathematical procedure appropriate for revealing significant relationships between the judge's voting record and his

---

[15] See p. 1557 *supra*.

"personal values and attitudes." We must appraise the findings and decide what use we can make of them. At each of these turning points the researcher, I must insist, has nothing more "scientific" to guide him than his own imperfect insight into workings of the human mind and the human will.

III

It is time now to view the application of "predictive science" to judicial behavior from a somewhat broader perspective. In what kinds of situations in general is it possible to make reasonably reliable predictions of future human behavior?

Frank H. Knight [16] offers a comparison that may be useful in giving a partial answer to this question — a partial answer extremely relevant to our present subject. Suppose I observe someone else working on a problem. Now if I have myself previously reached a satisfactory solution for this problem, I may be able within limits to predict the outcome of his attempts to solve it. But if the problem is as much a problem for me as it is for him, plainly I cannot know in advance what is going to emerge from his efforts.

The question then becomes whether the judicial office involves a problem-solving aspect. Certainly lawyers talk all the time as if it did. "That decision was a very good solution for a tough problem." "Judge X certainly messed that one up." "An opinion supporting that conclusion, I found when I tried it, just wouldn't write." "That's a decision we can live with."

As a judge or arbitrator sitting in the case of *A. v. B.* I may think I intuitively perceive that justice lies on the side of *B.* But if I cannot bring to articulation the reasons for this perception, I shall be unable to state a clear rule that will give meaningful guidance to those compelled to shape their conduct by my decision. If I must fit an apt decision of the case into an existing body of precedent my perplexities are compounded. I must avoid the opposing perils of a wooden literalness and an unprincipled manipulation of the sense of existing doctrine. Knowing that my decision will in turn become a precedent, I must find an apt decision of the case before me without compromising the decision of cases yet to come and as yet unforeseeable.

---

[16] See KNIGHT, THE ETHICS OF COMPETITION AND OTHER ESSAYS 340 n.† (1951).

The great judges of the past are not celebrated because they displayed in their judicial "votes" dispositions congenial to later generations. Rather their fame rests on their ability to devise apt, just, and understandable rules of law; they are held up as models because they were able to bring to clear expression thoughts that in lesser minds would have remained too vague and confused to serve as adequate guideposts for human conduct. Thus one recent writer says of certain of the great chancellors of England: ". . . one is struck by the power which these judges showed to subsume complicated commercial situations under the comparatively simple rules of equity so as to arrive at a result which satisfies one's sense of justice." [17]

It would be foolish to assert that when judges are engaged in solving problems all of their personal attitudes and values become dissipated in a bright glow of objectivity. The final solution may well be skewed in one direction or another by something that may be termed a personal or collegial predilection. But plainly this does not mean that the predictive social scientist will be able to anticipate the outcome; indeed, he will not even be able to identify the skew until the structure subject to it stands before him and he is able to comprehend its meaning. Furthermore, there are cases — and they are by no means rare — where the judge may be able to devise a solution that will reconcile and bring into harmony interests that were previously in conflict. Such a solution offers no handles at all to the social scientist who draws his premises from an assumption of ineluctable conflict.

The studies reported in Grossman's paper are the work of scholars who are by profession political scientists. Grossman recognizes that they bring a distinct point of view to their researches: [18]

> They rely on methods of inquiry which assume that a useful way to examine judicial behavior is to consider the judge not as *sui generis*, but rather as a variety of *homo politicus*. Such a perspective is not to be confused with the exaggerated notion that judges are *no* different from other political actors. It has the advantage, however, of permitting observations about judicial behavior to be integrated into broader-based studies of human behavior and legal-political institutions.

---

[17] Kahn-Freund, *Comparative Law as an Academic Subject*, 82 L.Q. Rev. 40, 46 (1966).

[18] See p. 1552 *supra* (footnote omitted).

If the broader perspective thus offered leads us to think of judicial "voting" as being fundamentally like the casting of his ballot by an ordinary citizen, it will certainly serve no purpose but obfuscation. The *homo politicus* nearest in function to the judge is, perhaps, the elected representative in a legislative assembly. Like the judge he not only votes for or against legal measures but also participates in their construction. Unlike the judge he performs these two functions separately; the one takes place "on the floor," the other in committee. The struggle of interests and viewpoints that comes to open expression on the floor is by no means absent in the committee. A bill may be killed or mutilated in the drafting stage by the pressure of powerful political interests. On the other hand, laws are sometimes proposed that seem certain of wide support, that promise an end to partisan strife — until someone tries to draft them. Tax exemptions in certain situations of hardship that sound very good on paper ("off-paper" would be a better expression) sometimes prove themselves undraftable in any way that would not cause confusion and damaging uncertainty.

With the judge the drafting and voting stages are not clearly differentiated and commonly proceed in parallel. This difference easily leads to a misunderstanding of the judicial process. For example, a dissenting opinion is not necessarily a vote "against" the majority view. In legislative parlance it may be more like an expression of the opinion that the decision is not yet ready to be reported out of committee.

None of this is intended to deny that the judicial office can bring to expression both capacities for problem-solving and individual differences in fundamental values. One may, indeed, distinguish in the judicial process two aspects, the one consisting of what may be called signpost-setting, the other of constructing roadways to the destinations indicated by the signs. Just as there are legislators who are magnificent on the floor and weak in committee, so there are judges who are very adept in setting signposts but less effective in road construction. One sometimes has the uncomfortable feeling that these are the favorites of the predictors. Certainly such judges offer more tractable material for their researches.

In one of the most significant actions of the Supreme Court in this century we have had the unusual experience of seeing the signpost-setting and the roadbuilding aspects of the judicial office neatly separated. *Baker v. Carr* [19] set the signpost; *Reynolds v. Sims* [20] took up the work of constructing the roadway. The route is far from being completely charted; much of the terrain that lies ahead has hardly been scanned. Difficult problems remain to be solved.

Interestingly enough, certain political scientists are now hard at work attempting to solve these problems in some acceptably objective way. As one of their number has observed: "The difficulties are not only political; some of them are technical." [21] The most difficult problem is to find some formula for redrafting the boundaries of election districts in ways that will not produce bizarre configurations and yet avoid the evil of inconspicuous gerrymandering. To that end there have been developed what are called the Weaver-Hess program and the Nagel program. These programs, which involve the use of computers, are projected against a body of learning that includes the Dauer-Kelsay and Gini indexes and the Schutz coefficient. One may wish these scientists Godspeed in their labors. Of one thing we can be reasonably sure, however: it is unlikely that their colleagues, the predictors, will attempt at this stage to forecast the ultimate results of their efforts at problem solving. In the case of Stuart Nagel, himself an eminent predictor, this would have involved predicting from the beginning the outcome of his own efforts as a problem solver.

Throughout this article we have been concerned to identify the abstractions and simplifications implicit in the design of research devoted to the prediction of judicial behavior. We have listed: (1) a selection of the factors to be tested for their influence on judicial behavior; (2) a definition of "outcomes" which excludes unanimous decisions and gives a heavy weighting to dissents and dissenting opinions; (3) a determination of what particular judicial "votes" shall be taken to mean in terms of objectives pursued in the research; and (4) the choice of a mathematical method for bringing into significant relationship the influences that may sway a judge and the decisions he actually makes. We may now add: (5) an exclusion from study of the problem-solving aspect of the judicial process.

[19] 369 U.S. 186 (1962).

[20] 377 U.S. 533 (1964).

[21] Silva, *Reapportionment and Redistricting*, Scientific American, Nov. 1965, pp. 20–27. The summary of the work now going on, presented in the text above, is based on this article.

In apology for the unexciting findings of these researches it is often claimed for them that they at least serve to confirm by scientific methods what we previously knew only intuitively. This claim is not, I believe, justified. The success achieved in proving the intuitively obvious is built into the design of the research itself.

IV

We now reach the most fundamental question of all: What are the ultimate aims of research of the kind we have been discussing? What philosophy animates it? What imparted sense of mission enables it to attract to itself so many man hours and such extensive facilities?

Not much by way of practical utility has been claimed for it. In an article addressed to lawyers Stuart Nagel attempts to outline briefly the kind of practical guidance that might be obtained from the conclusions of predictive research:[22]

> Knowing the rough probability of victory in cases before the Supreme Court might be helpful in rationing scarce resources or revising the briefs of a law firm, a pressure group, or the solicitor general's office, although even if one has a case that falls into the [unpromising] extreme intervals in Table 2, it may still be worth participating in an appeal if the gain to be achieved in case of victory is enough to offset the low probability of victory, or if there is some special characteristic present that indicates the probability of victory is much higher than calculated (*e.g.*, the other side had no standing to sue).

One might add, as a reason for taking the long-shot case, that if the Court has fallen into predictably routine patterns of decision it might be in the public interest for a good lawyer to step in and shake them loose from their bureaucratic rigidities. But even as thus expanded the claim of practical utility remains a modest one. Indeed, an unkind critic might turn Nagel's reference to "rationing scarce resources" against a scientific enterprise that seems to return so little from so much.

Another possible gain from researches of this kind lies in the realm of serendipity. A puzzling correlation that violates normal anticipations may set our minds going along new paths and yield unexpected insights. If it is true that computers have the capacity

---

[22] Nagel, *supra* note 1, at 1421.

to think only to the extent that thinkers build that capacity into them, it is also true that much of what we call thinking is not thinking at all. It might better be called scanning; we force our brains to survey a long list of possibilities on the off-chance that some significant relationship will turn up. This disagreeable labor the computers can take over for us and perform with superhuman speed and precision. The trouble here is that our predictors of judicial behavior draw up such timid and conservative lists of factors to be tested. Perhaps if their minds could be made bolder, and the new spirit communicated to the inner offices of the foundations, some hitherto unsuspected aspects of judicial motivation might be opened up for investigation. But the hope for any such development must lie in the future.

As matters now stand, it seems obvious that the real driving force back of these researches lies in the faith, or the hope, that they will ultimately make some as yet unspecifiable contribution to a General Science of Human Behavior. This faith, or hope, comes to clear expression in Grossman's article:[23]

> All research must be understood and interpreted in the light of the organizing principles to which it subscribes. The ultimate goals of social science involve the construction of sophisticated theories of human behavior, in which judicial processes occupy a small but important part. Such theories emphasize systematic formulations of empirical data and place a high premium on generalization and prediction. It may be, as Schubert suggests, that "the power of any science lies in its capacity to make successful predictions." But successful prediction alone is not what distinguishes scientific endeavor. Scholars and ordinary people are constantly making predictions — some with greater success than others. The scientist seeks prediction based objectively on the measurement of relationships of observed data; to most people, and often to scientists as well, prediction is intuitive and based on less than complete data. It is this goal of more objectivity and increased reliability of prediction and inference which supplies the major motivation for much of the work described below.

In these words — which will bear careful reading — there lies implicit a whole philosophy of scientific method. I believe this philosophy to be mistaken. In what follows I shall try to show why I believe this.

There may be said to exist two philosophies of science. The one

---

[23] P. 1553 *supra* (footnotes omitted).

sees the aim of science as *understanding*; the other as *prediction*. The first regards prediction as a by-product of understanding; we acquire the ability to predict events as our minds penetrate into the causes that underlie the happenings of nature. The adherents of the opposed theory see "understanding" as an illusory, metaphysical trapping superfluously tacked on the essential goal of acquiring predictive knowledge.

It may be said of the great scientists of history that they generally pursued their goals of discovery without imposing on themselves preconceived limitations of method. Insofar as they had a philosophy of method it would probably resemble, if brought to articulation, that which I have described as attributing to science the aim of understanding.

The adherents of the predictive theory have always been more self-conscious about their beliefs and at times have formed something like a cult. The basic elements of their faith can be traced through Bacon, Comte, Mach, Poincaré, Pearson, and many others, including Holmes and his celebrated "predictive theory of law." In modern times the chief adherents of this view have been social scientists and certain philosophers of science. It has never had much attraction for those actively engaged in the physical sciences.

Let me first state the chief arguments for the predictive theory. It is recalled that the whole history of science is a graveyard of abandoned theories that were once thought to yield "explanations." In ancient times explanatory power was attributed to the principle that "nature abhors a vacuum." At a later time the imaginary substance *phlogiston* was once as real in the thinking of chemists as oxygen is today. What persisted through these shifts of fashion in explanation was a steadily increasing knowledge of invariant sequences: when *a* occurs then *b* follows. This, it is said, is the bedrock of scientific knowledge. This conception of the scientific enterprise has in recent times become attractive because of its pragmatic flavor. It is now sometimes stated as a view that sees the essence of science in prediction *and control*. In any event, it emphasizes action, not passive contemplation.

A general answer from the opposing side would run along these lines. Prediction presupposes understanding. In the sequence — when *a* occurs *b* follows — often we cannot even identify *a* or *b* except by some perceived structure or causal connection which unites them. The acquisition of significant scientific insight does not necessarily increase our capacity to predict. One of the most revolutionary developments in the history of science — Darwin's theory of natural selection — did not yield predictions. That the constructs on which men once relied in explaining what they observed have often been abandoned later in no sense refutes the theory that science seeks understanding. Many tools that were once the best available have been supplanted by more effective ones; this does not mean that the supplanted tools were not useful in their time. The predictive theory gives no guidance to scientific research. One who took it seriously would not know where to direct his inquiries. When the scientist seeks understanding, on the other hand, he starts with what he understands, or thinks he understands, and builds out from this into the unknown.

Certain modern philosophers have had occasion to refine and perfect the predictive theory of science. In defending that theory against its critics, they have clarified its claims and its limits. I think it is not generally realized by social scientists what the results of this process of clarification have been. The most significant of these is the conclusion that *the predictive theory offers no guidance whatsoever to the process of discovery.*

Carl C. Hempel is one of the most famous of those philosophers of science whose work falls generally within what may be called the predictive school. The logician Ernest Nagel thus summarizes the aims of Hempel's efforts:[24] "Hempel's main objective is to analyse the *logical structure* of scientific explanation rather than to examine the *process* of scientific discovery or the *development* of scientific ideas."

Another member of the same school of thought, Hans Reichenbach, has this to say of his own objectives:[25]

> The act of discovery escapes logical analysis; there are no logical rules in terms of which a "discovery machine" could be constructed that would take over the creative function of the genius. But it is not the logician's task to account for scientific discoveries; all he can do is to analyze the relation between given facts and a theory presented to him with the claim that it explains these facts. In other words, logic is concerned only with the context of justification.

Much of the popularity that the predictive conception now enjoys among social scientists can be attributed to the attractive

---

[24] Letter, Scientific American, April 1966, p. 8, col. 2.

[25] REICHENBACH, THE RISE OF SCIENTIFIC PHILOSOPHY 231 (1951). The quotation is taken from a chapter entitled "Predictive Knowledge."

aura of scientific objectivity surrounding Holmes's "predictive theory of law." Yet Holmes never gave any significant indication as to how anyone would actually go about making the predictions which occupy so central a position in his theory. The only advice he offers cannot be said to suffer from an excess of imagination: "Read the reports, treatises, and statutes." [26]

What in fact has given direction to the researches of the great scientists of the past? I think it can be said that they usually started by trying to place in order what in their times seemed already well established and clearly understood. In this process of putting together the materials of familiar knowledge they would be likely to encounter conflicts and discordances. "We know from the Bible that God created the different kinds of animals, giving to each its special stamp. Yet we also know that stock breeders bring new kinds of animals into existence. How can this be?" Again: "We know of course that when a material like wood burns it releases a substance that passes off into the air in the form of flames. Yet when we gather together and weigh all the products of combustion we find they are heavier than the wood was before it went up in flames. How can this be explained?" Guided then by a defect in existing knowledge, the nature of which he could not yet define, the scientist went on to discover a solution, the nature of which he could not anticipate.

Are there in our present subject any unresolved perplexities concealed in the interstices of what we take to be commonplace knowledge? There are indeed. The most obvious and central of these lies in our received conceptions of the means-end relation as it enters into processes of decision.

Let me set forth a series of propositions about means and ends that have, in whole or in part, some chance of being accepted as truisms: The first thing to do in reaching any decision is to determine what end you wish to achieve. This end must be clearly defined, for otherwise it will be impossible to select intelligently an apt means for attaining it. In setting up objectives or ends rational calculation is itself not enough. In determining what we wish ultimately to achieve we must be guided by some felt need, or by a sense of what is right and just, or simply by personal preference. The choice of means, on the other hand, is a matter of rational calculations. This results in the conclusion that science can help us with means, but not with ends.

---

[26] See Holmes, *The Path of the Law*, 10 HARV. L. REV. 457 (1897).

Trouble develops, however, when we attempt to apply this conventional wisdom — to borrow a phrase from Kenneth Galbraith — to actual processes of decision. Then we find means and ends moving in circles of reciprocal influence. An end originally selected may be discarded because no means can be found for achieving it that does not entail a disproportionate cost — a "cost" that may itself mean some sacrifice of other ends or the exclusion of means that would be useful in attaining a variety of ends. When in this field of interaction we try to isolate the ends that are "ultimate," we find ourselves in difficulty. The most hackneyed social aims — freedom, equality, security — can hardly be conceived in abstraction from the institutional means essential for achieving them. If we say that the ultimate commitment of a court passing on constitutional issues is to uphold and interpret the constitution, then we must remember that the constitution itself consists largely of a system of prescribed means. The end of the court then becomes that of preserving the integrity of a set of institutional means that must be kept open for the attainment of indeterminate ends. In actual processes of decision an end loosely defined and tentatively held may be more useful than one that seems clear and precise when viewed in abstraction from the reciprocal calculations into which it must eventually enter.

I do not mean to intimate that any discovery — and still less that any "scientific" discovery — lies around the corner that will enable us to straighten out all these tangles of thought. Perhaps the trouble lies not so much in lack of knowledge as in the lack of a language adequate to reflect the complexities of actual decisional processes. But meanwhile when we turn our minds to the process of decision we must not mistake an unreal model of that process for its realities.

In the studies under discussion a simplistic conception of the means-end relation reveals itself, I believe, in the neglect of the problem-solving aspect of the judicial process. The researchers have put an undue emphasis on what I have called signpost-setting as contrasted with road building. This is equivalent to saying that they have concentrated on judicial statements about ends to the neglect of judicial solutions for the problem of means. In judging the significance of this abstraction we must remember that majority and dissenting opinions are often parts of a continuing dialogue in which the signposts on both sides have to be readjusted from time to time to reflect the course of the roadway actually being constructed.

In a similar way I believe the researchers have been misled in forming their conception of scientific method. They have assumed that a goal that seems neat and clear, that of prediction, must in the nature of things be more useful than an obscure end like "understanding." They have forgotten that when they lose their way they will have to consult the wobbly needle of the compass called "understanding" to find out where they are.

In conclusion, my advice to the scholars whose work is reported in Grossman's article is that they should not set their sights so firmly on the distant goal of Predictive Science that they neglect the still imperfectly explored terrain that lies about them.

DATE DUE

GAYLORD			PRINTED IN U.S A